Real World
Colouring Book

For Advanced Users & Adults

50 Images

Created From Real Life Photos
For You To Colour As You Please.

ISBN 978-0-359-97225-8
90000
9 780359 972258

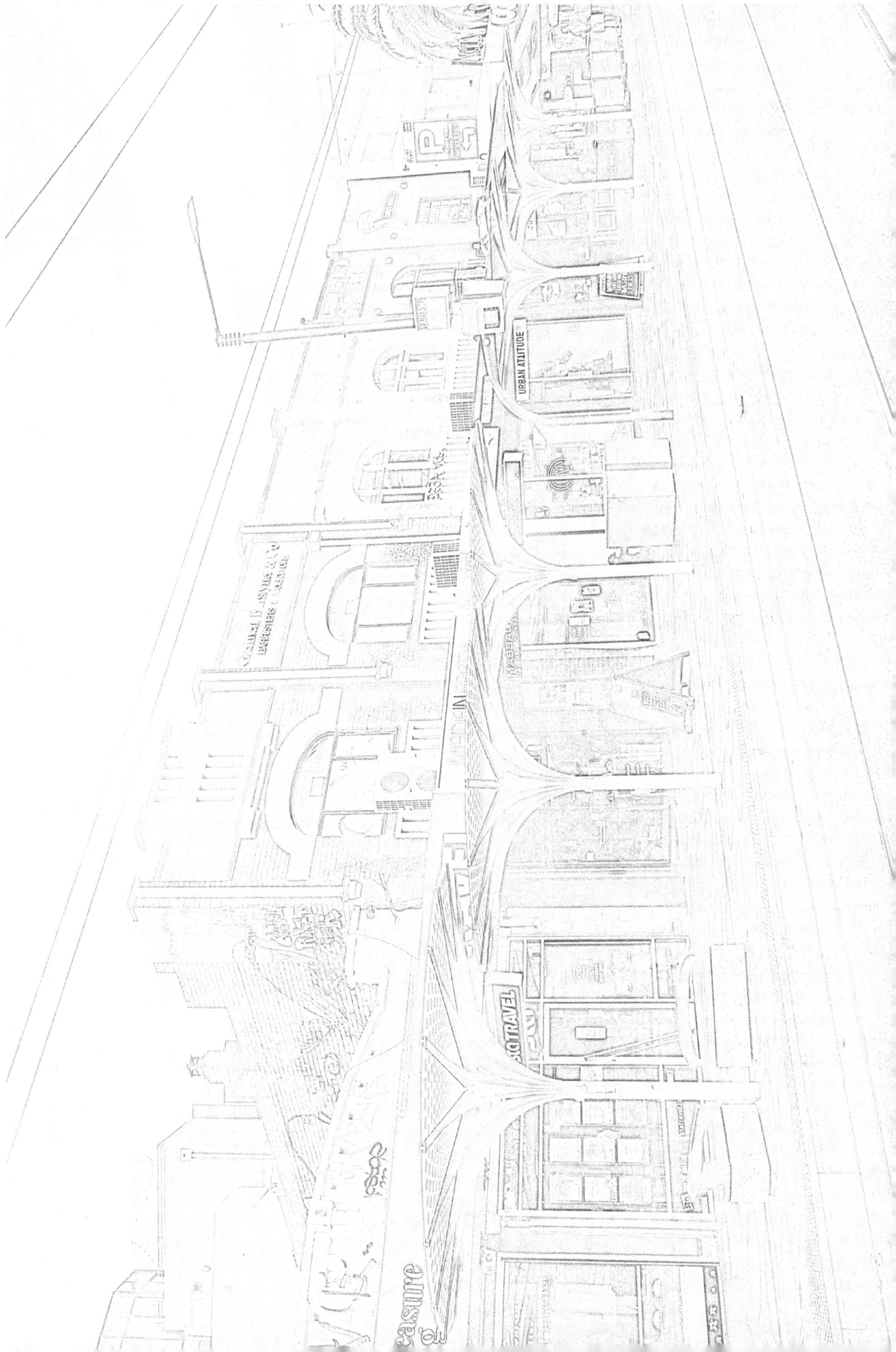
URBAN ATTITUDE

ACLAND COURT
coles
ACLAND COURT coles ACLAND COURT
ACLAND COURT
FOR LEASE
AREA 100 - 150 sqm
ALEXIA GATTI
0466 429 188
MICHAEL DI CARLO
0418 969 220
PT
Acland Street
Route To
East Brunswick via City
Platform 2
139
MAGNERS
priceline pharmacy
Tatts

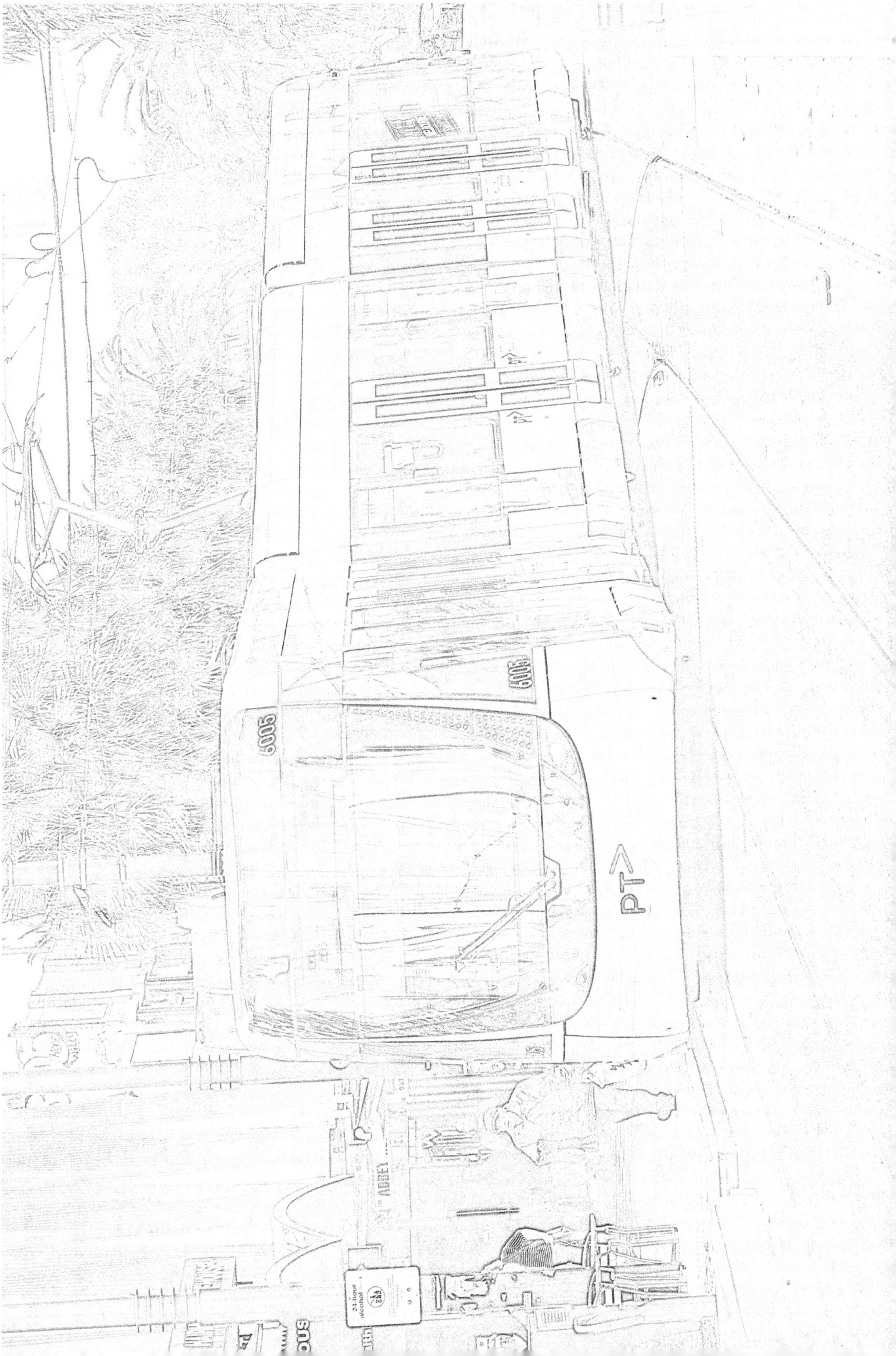
6005
6005
PT>
ABBEY
24-hour
alcohol

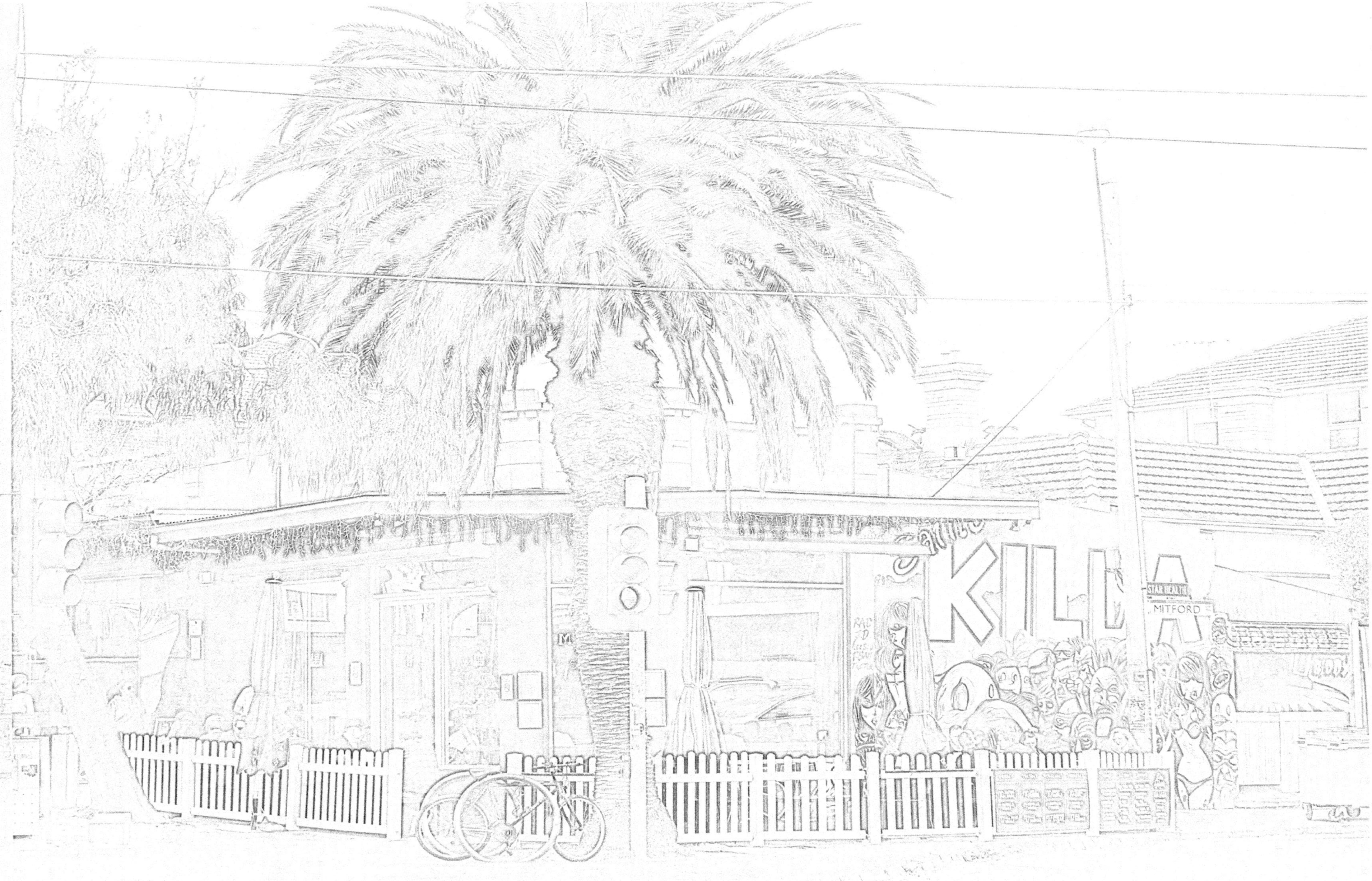
MITFORD

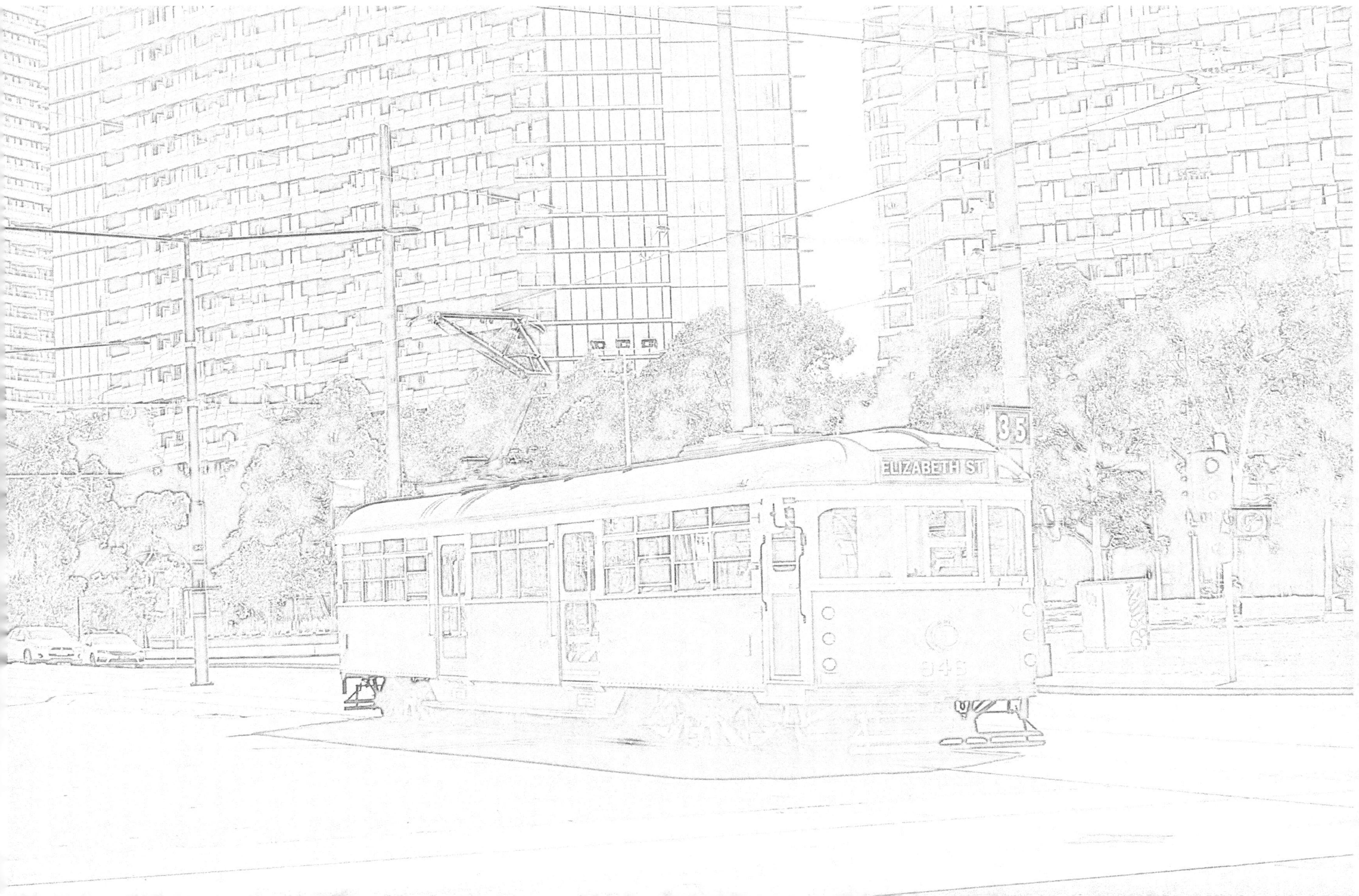
35
ELIZABETH ST

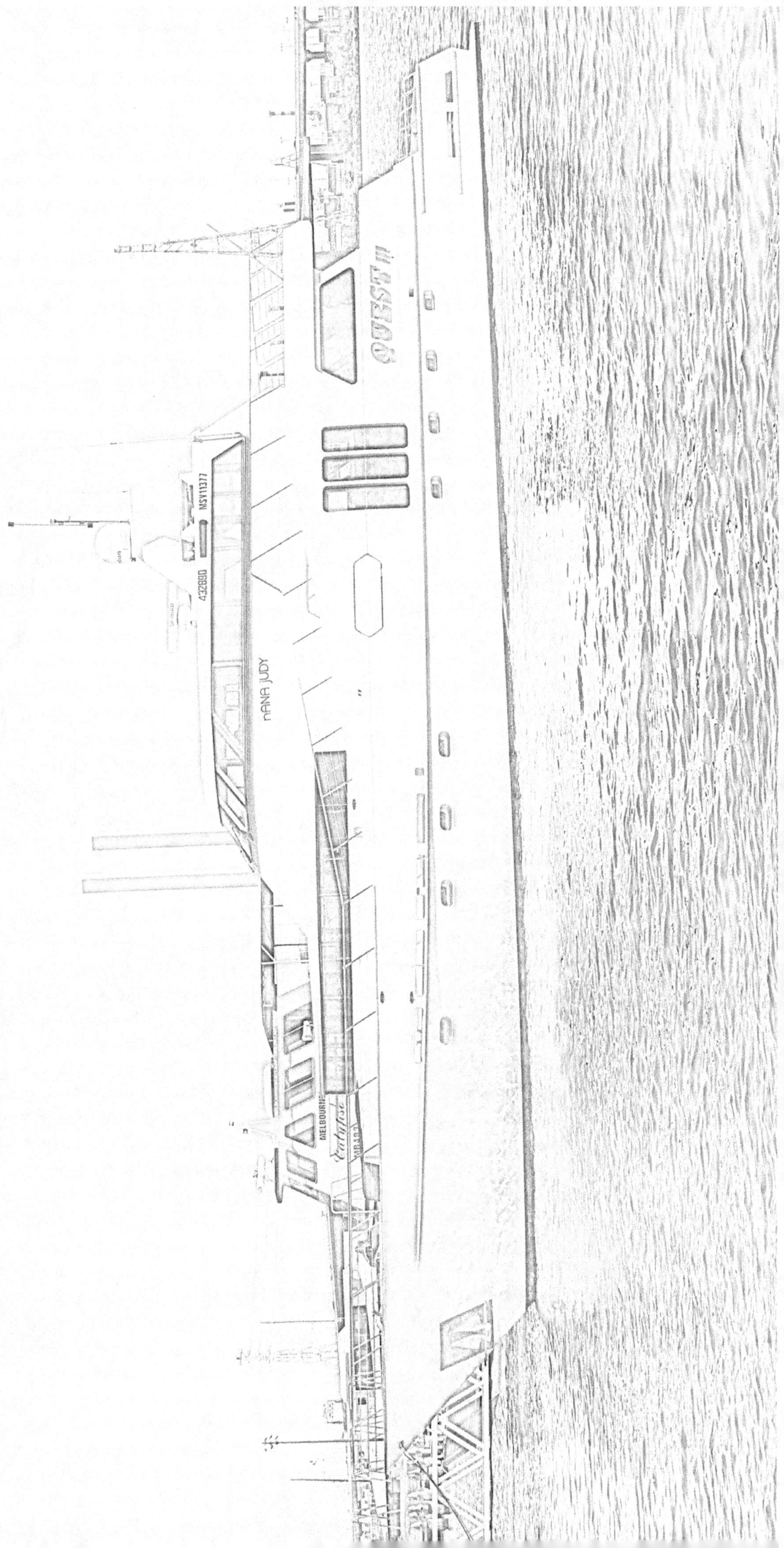
QUEST III
MSV11377
432890
NANA JUDY

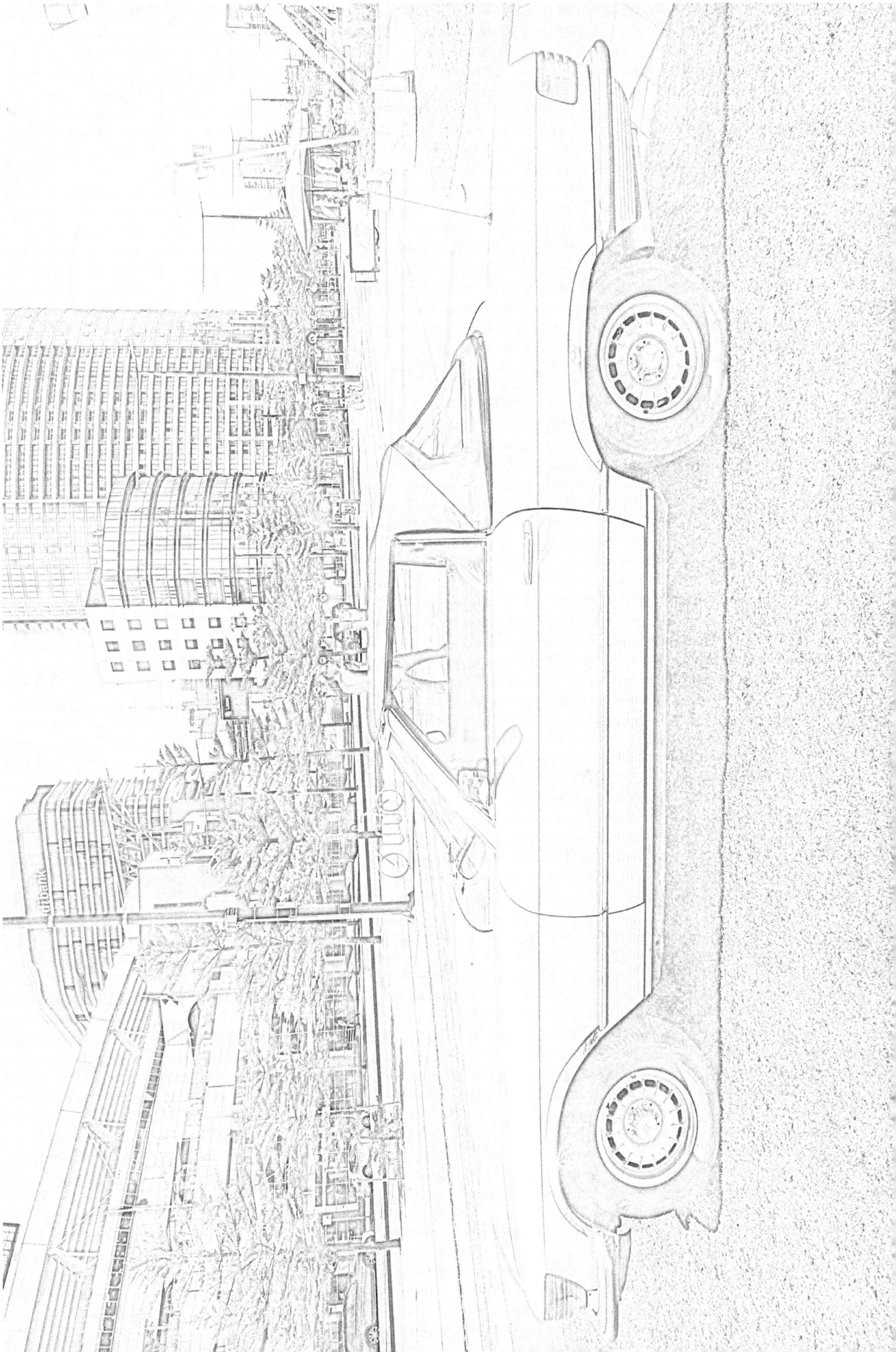

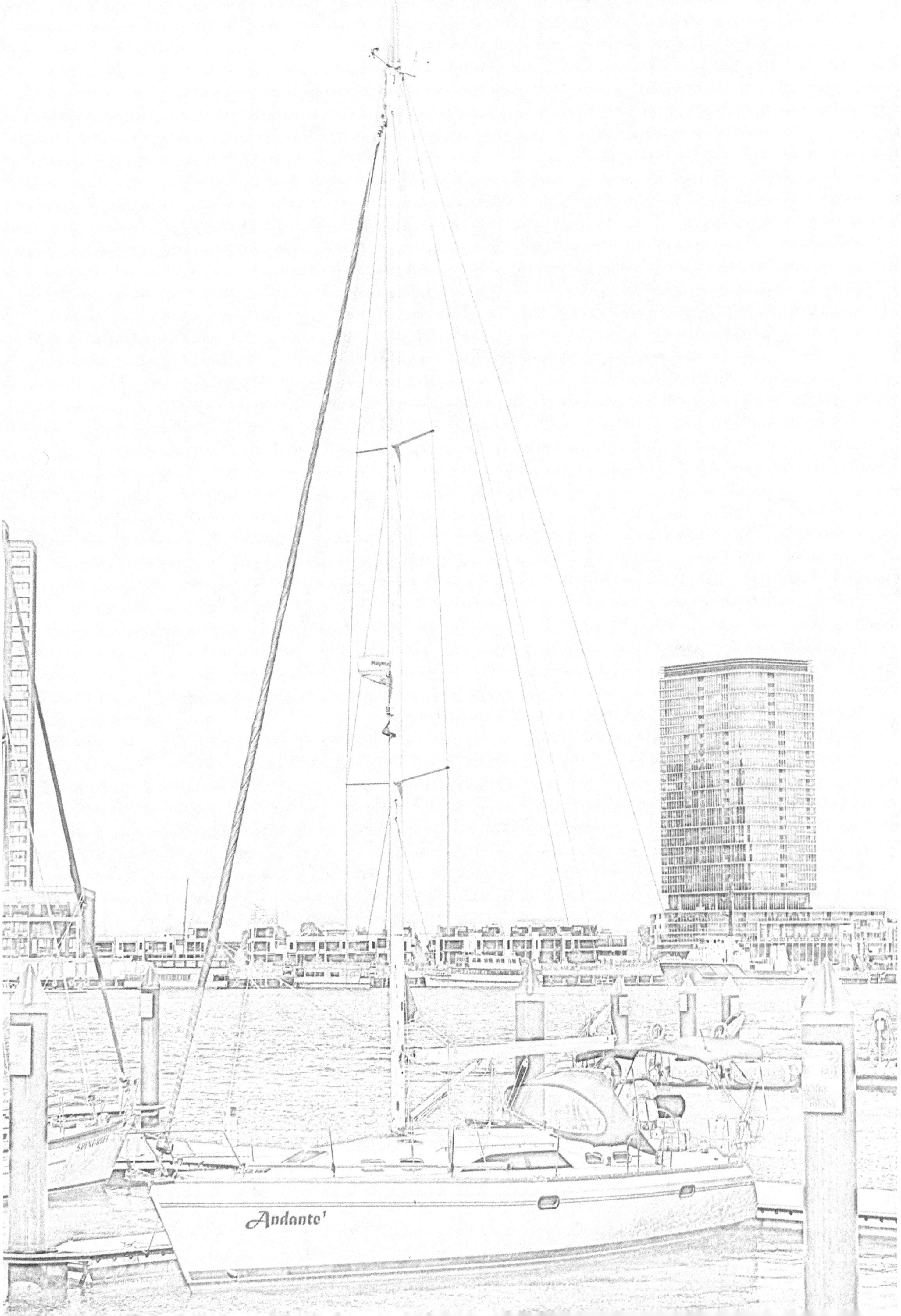
Andante'

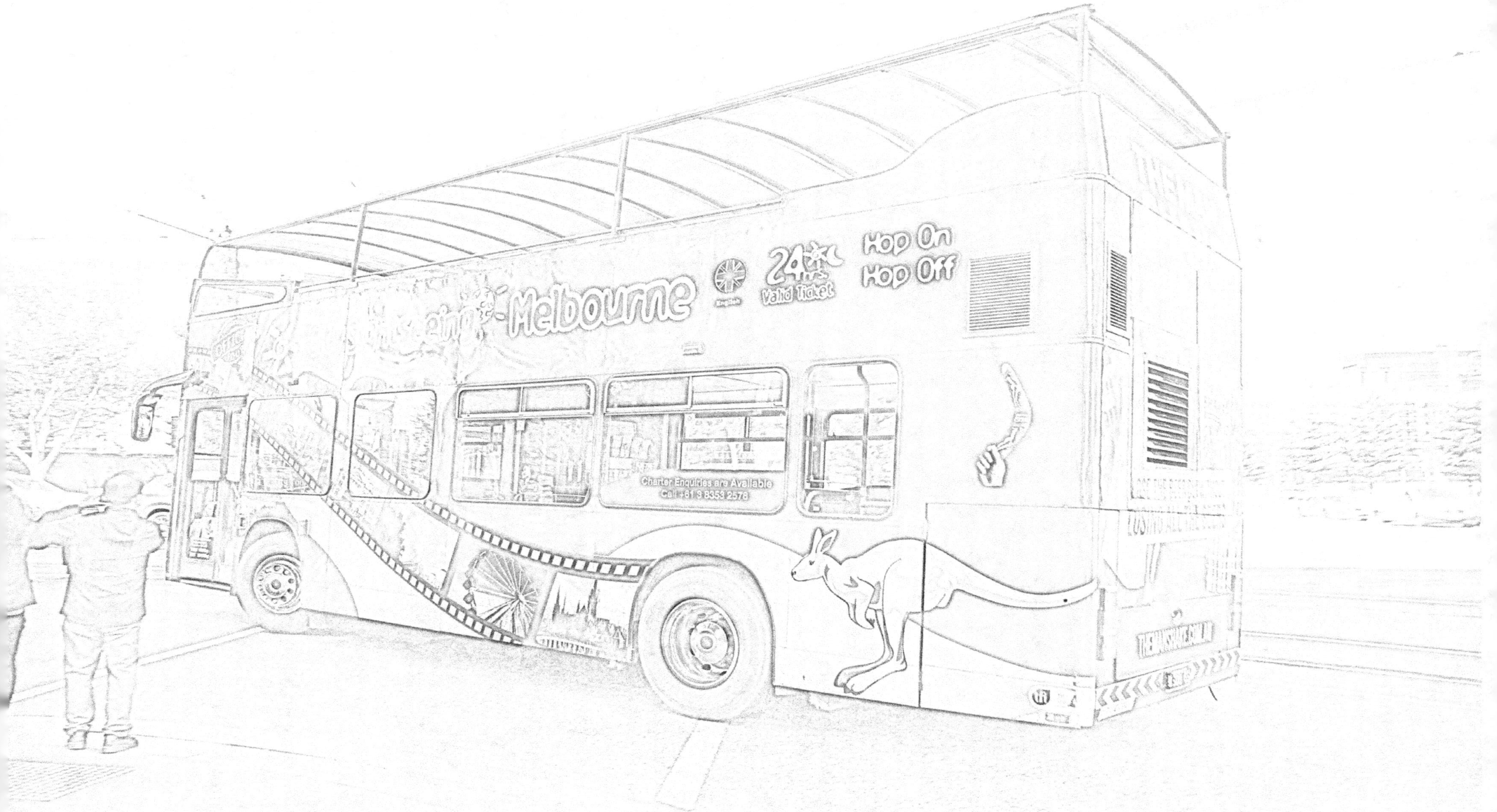
Melbourne
24 hrs Valid Ticket
Hop On
Hop Off
Charter Enquiries are Available
Call +61 3 8353 2578

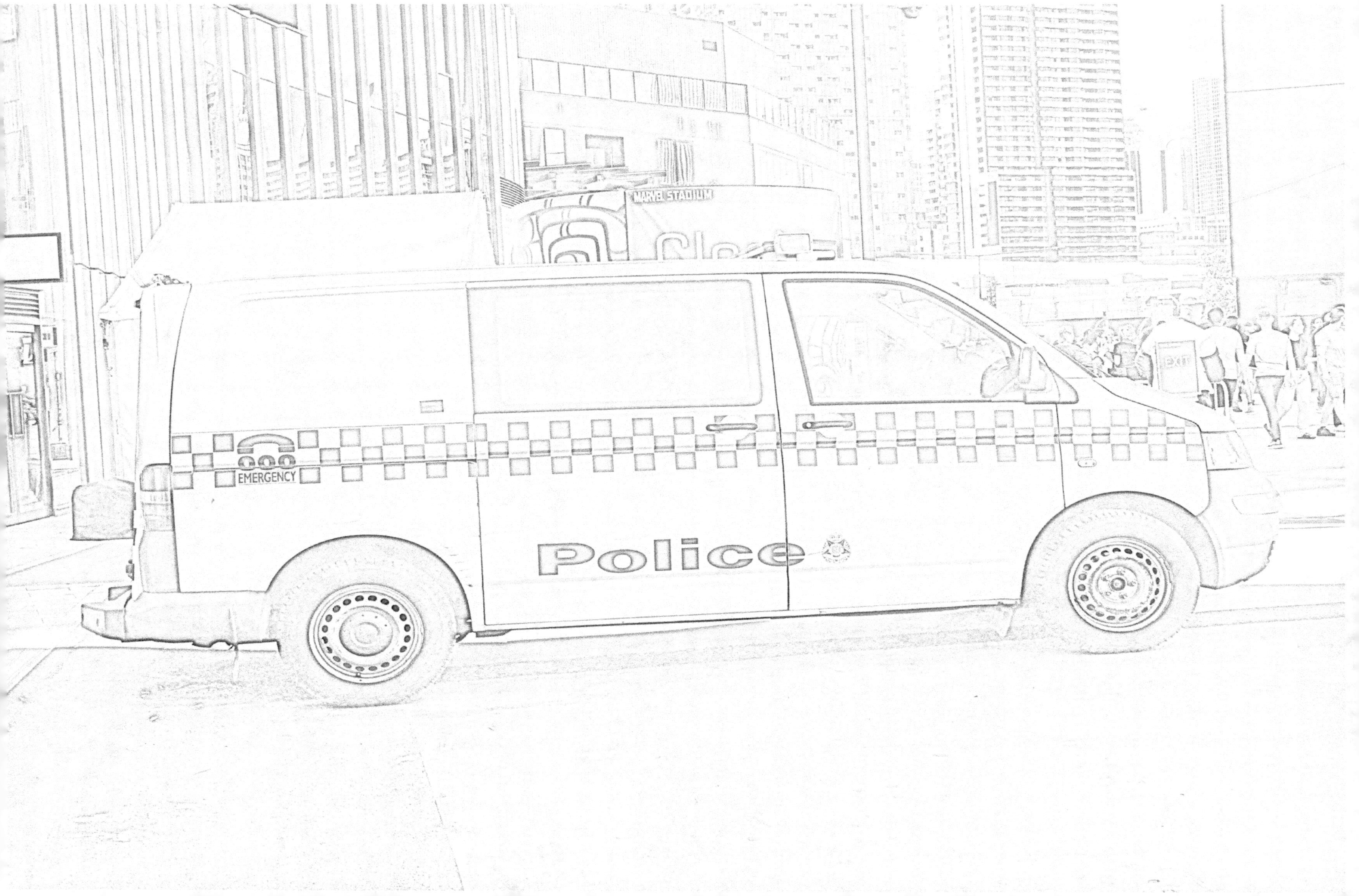
MARVEL STADIUM
EXIT
000
EMERGENCY
Police

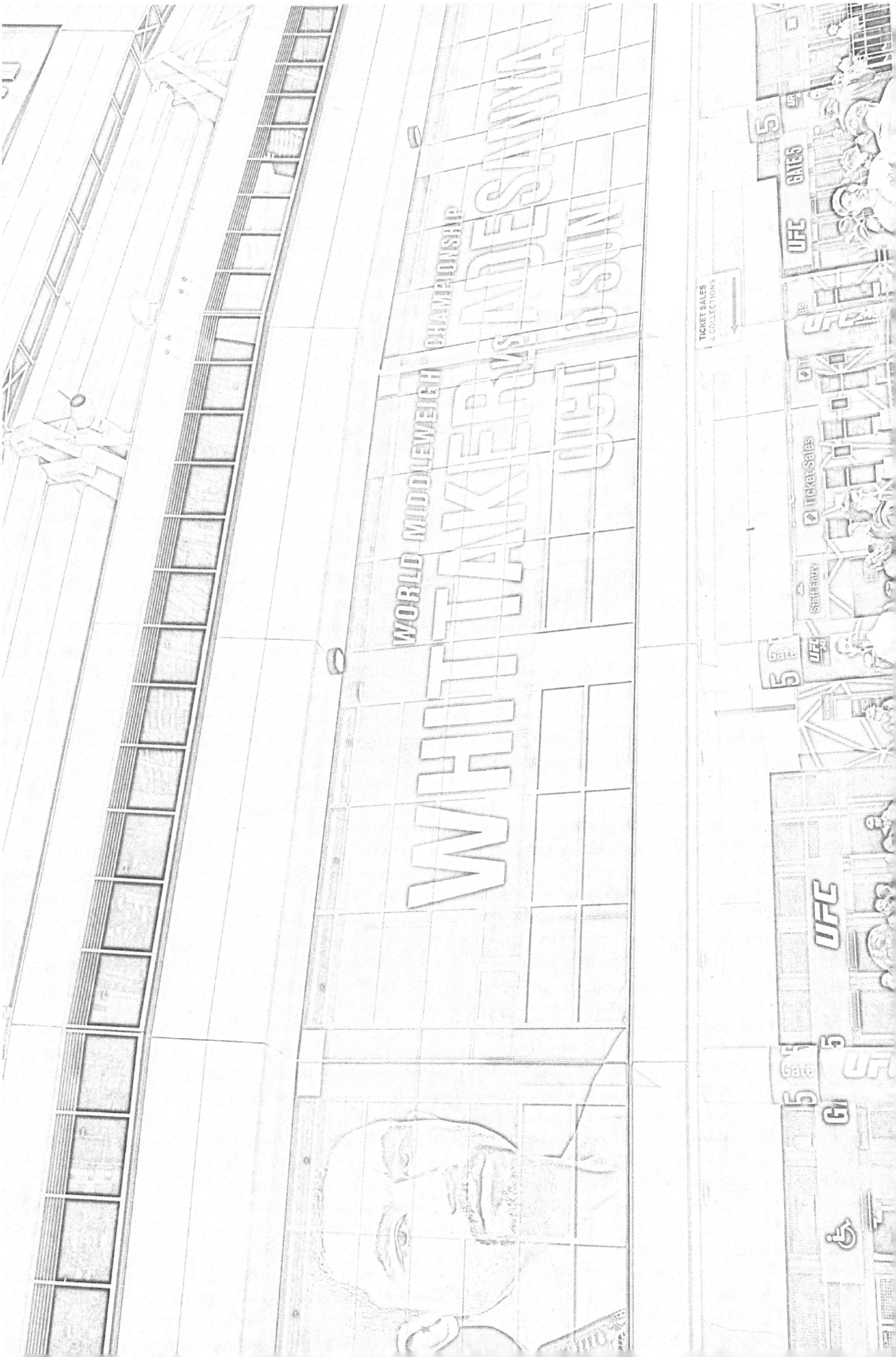
WORLD MIDDLEWEIGHT CHAMPIONSHIP
WHITTAKER vs ADESANYA
TICKET SALES & COLLECTIONS
Staff Entry
Ticket Sales
GATE 5
UFC

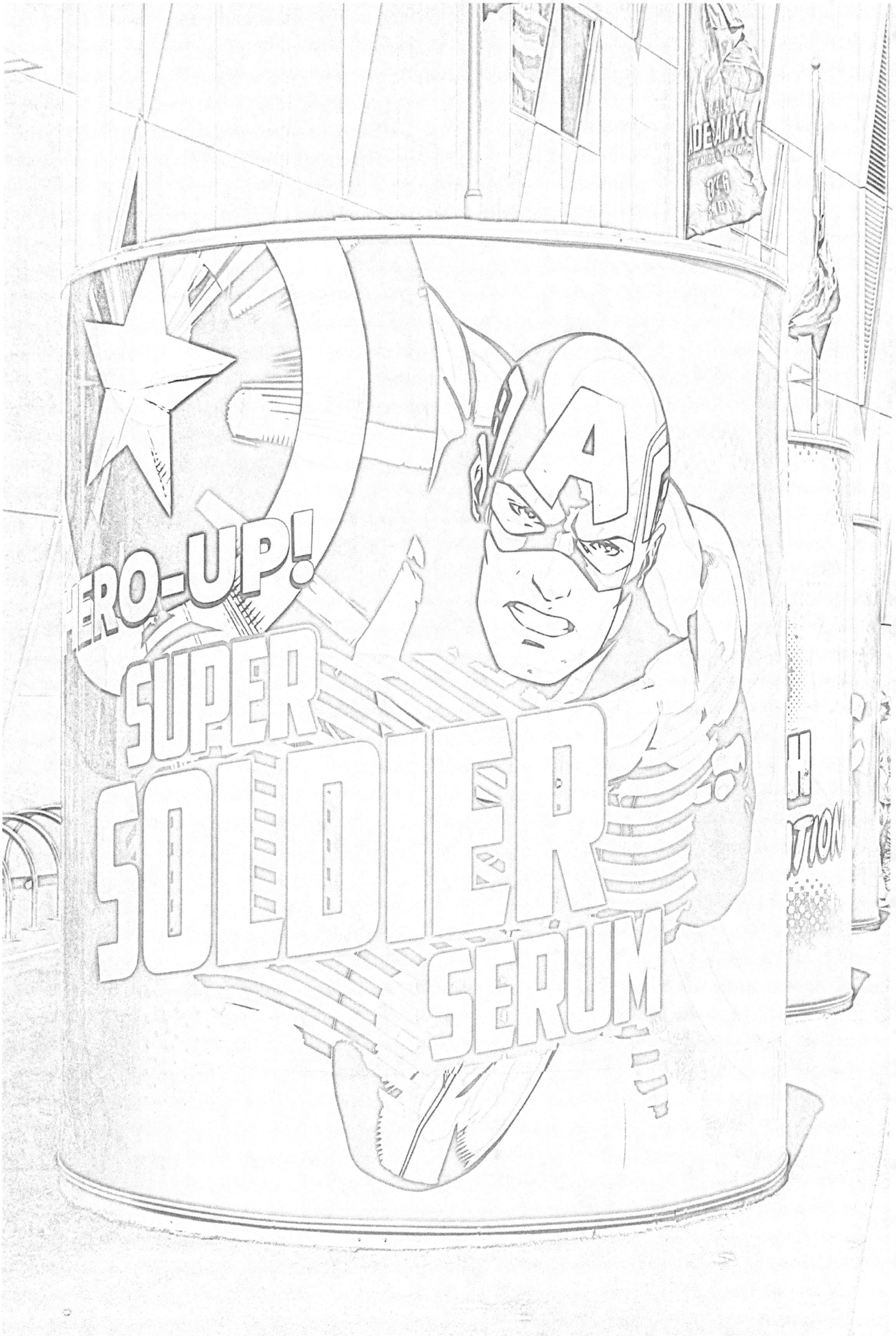
HERO-UP!
SUPER
SOLDIER
SERUM

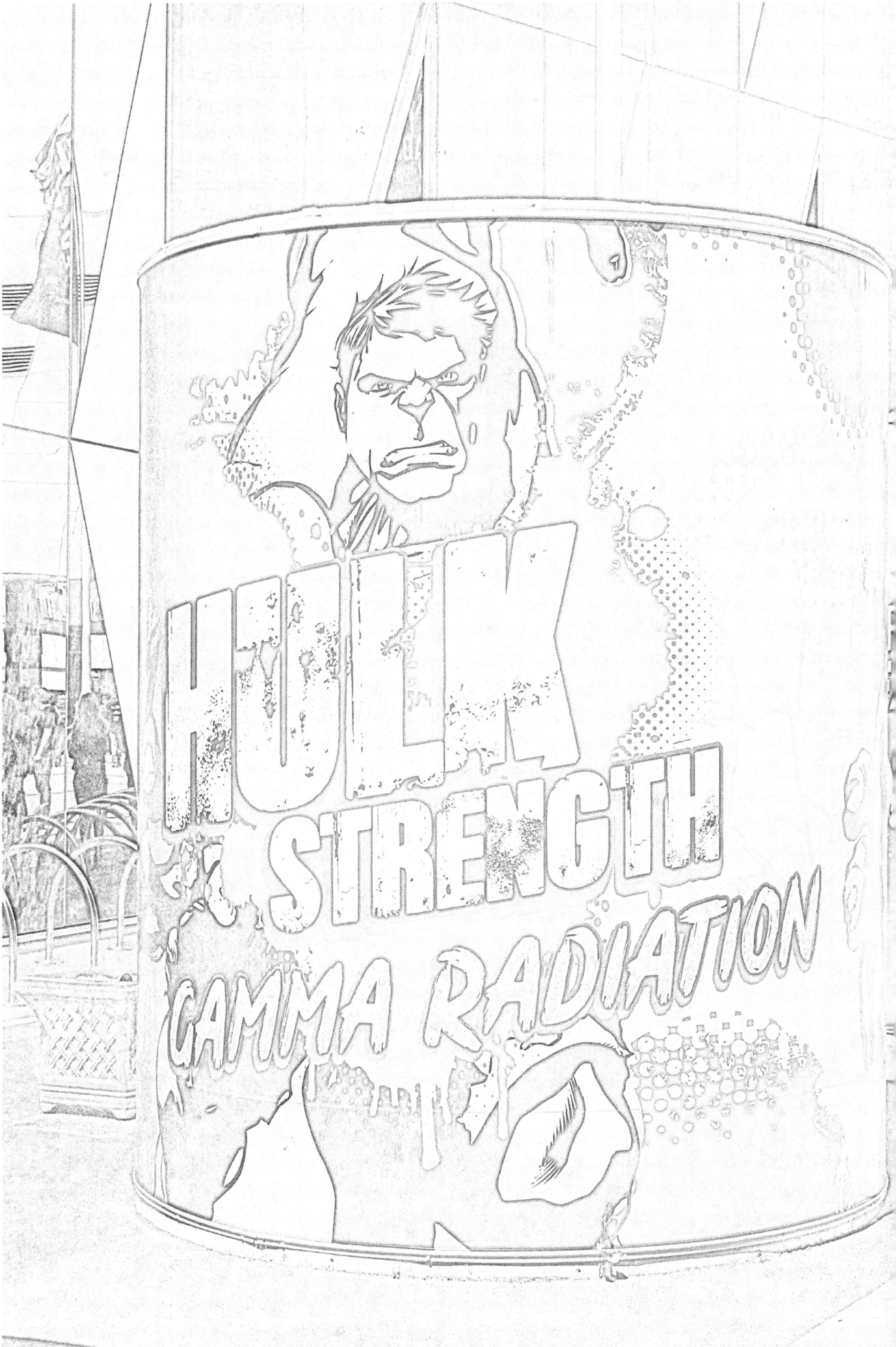
HULK
STRENGTH
GAMMA RADIATION

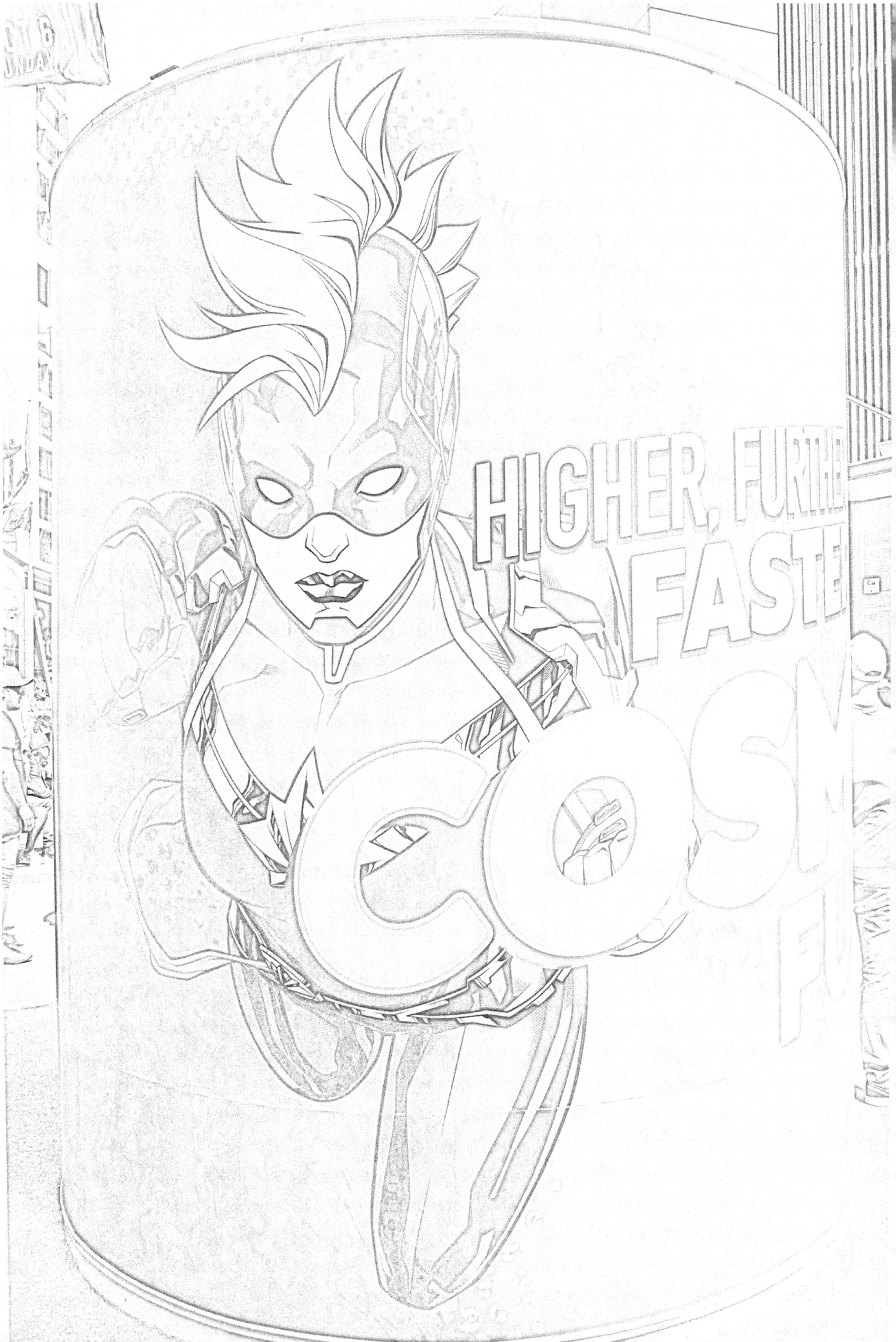
HIGHER,

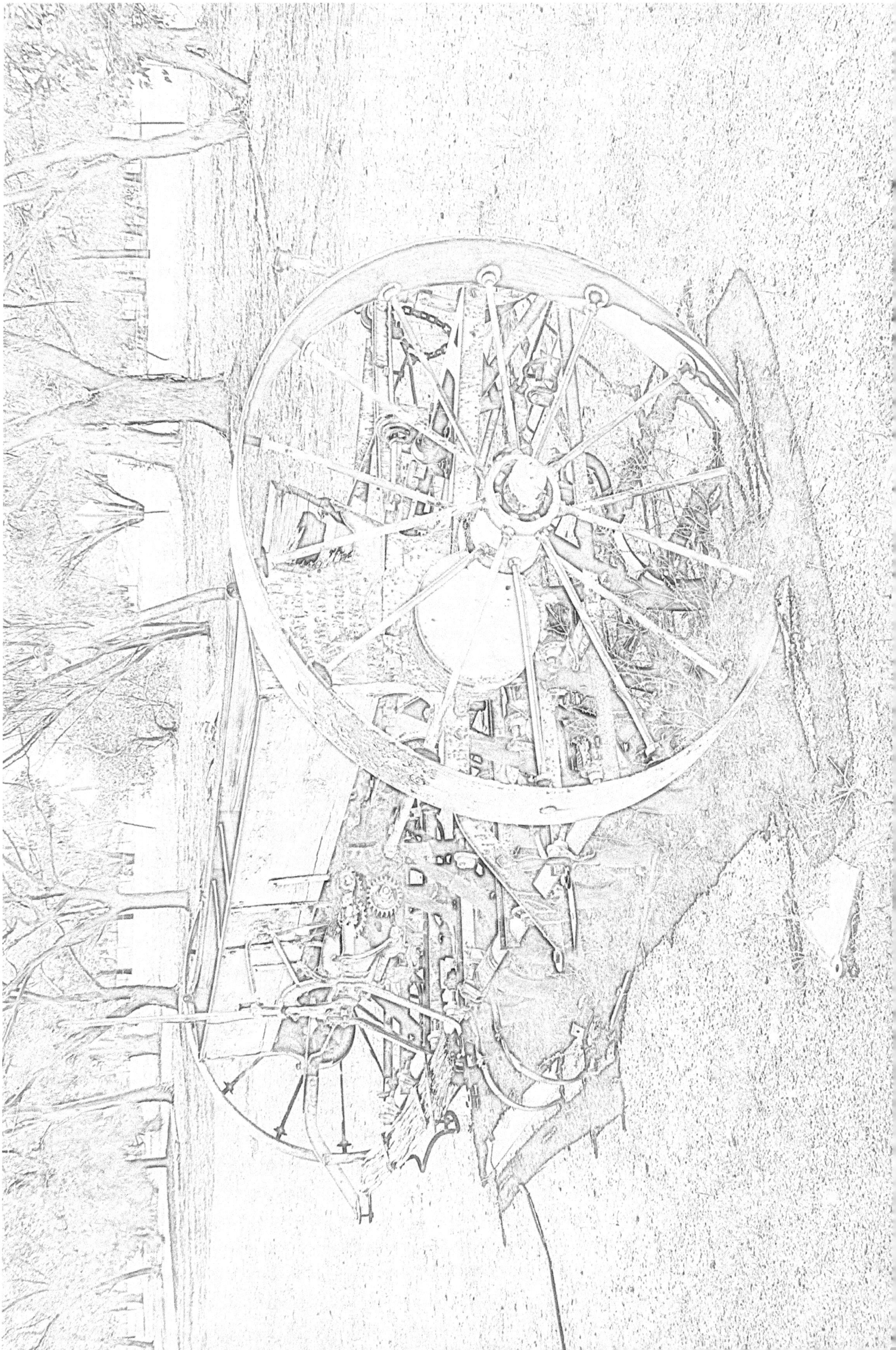

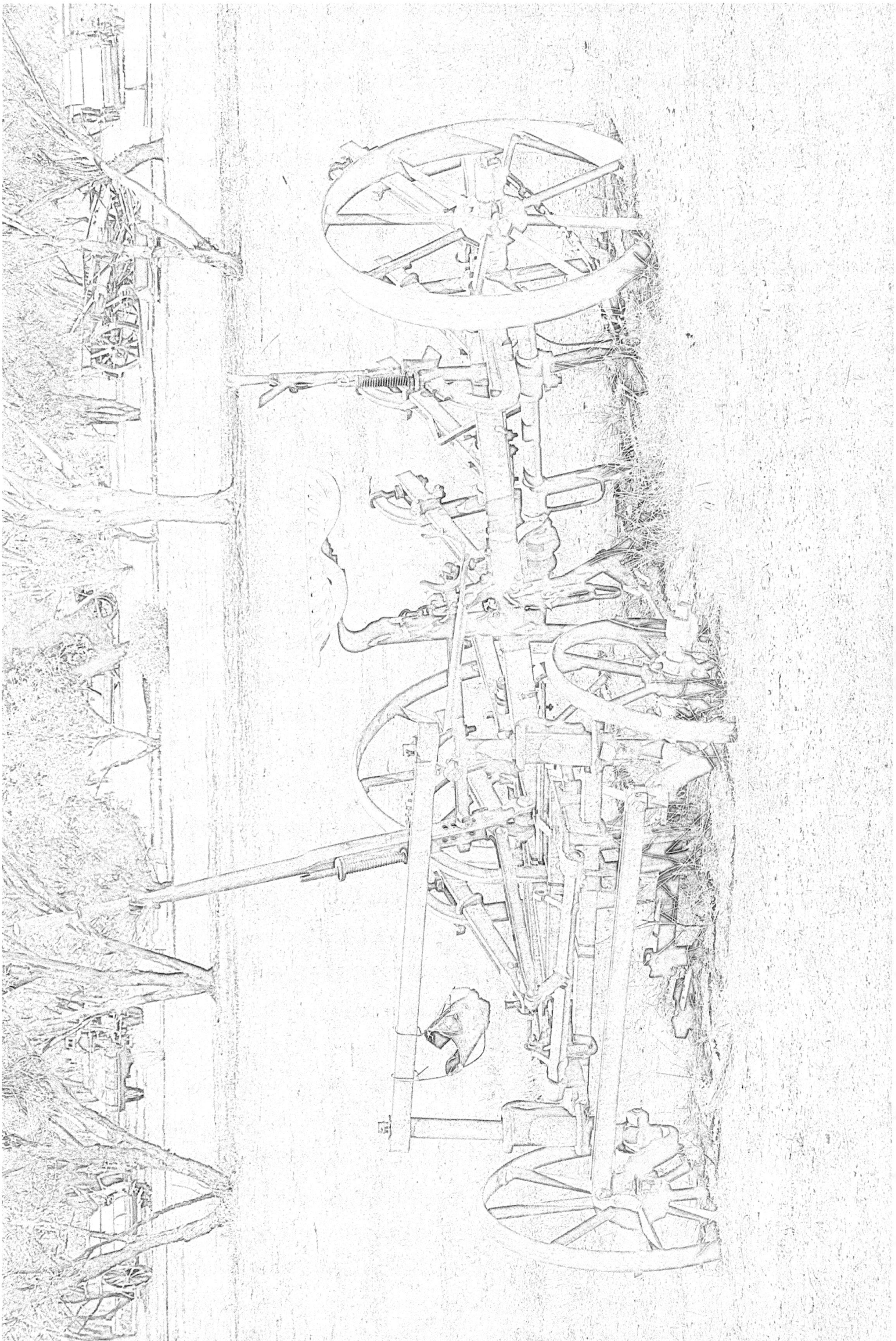

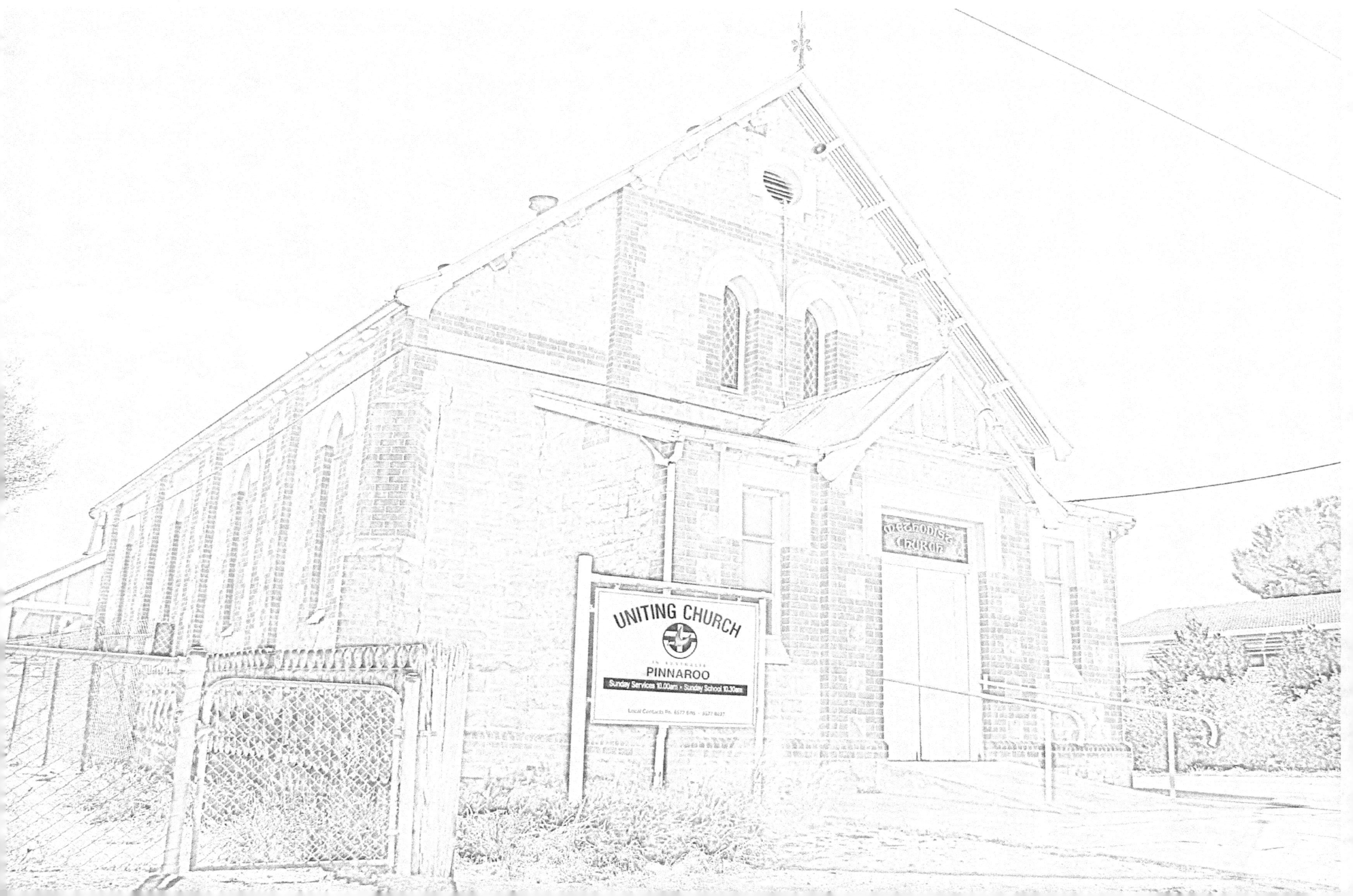
METHODIST CHURCH
UNITING CHURCH
PINNAROO
Sunday Services 10.00am • Sunday School 10.30am

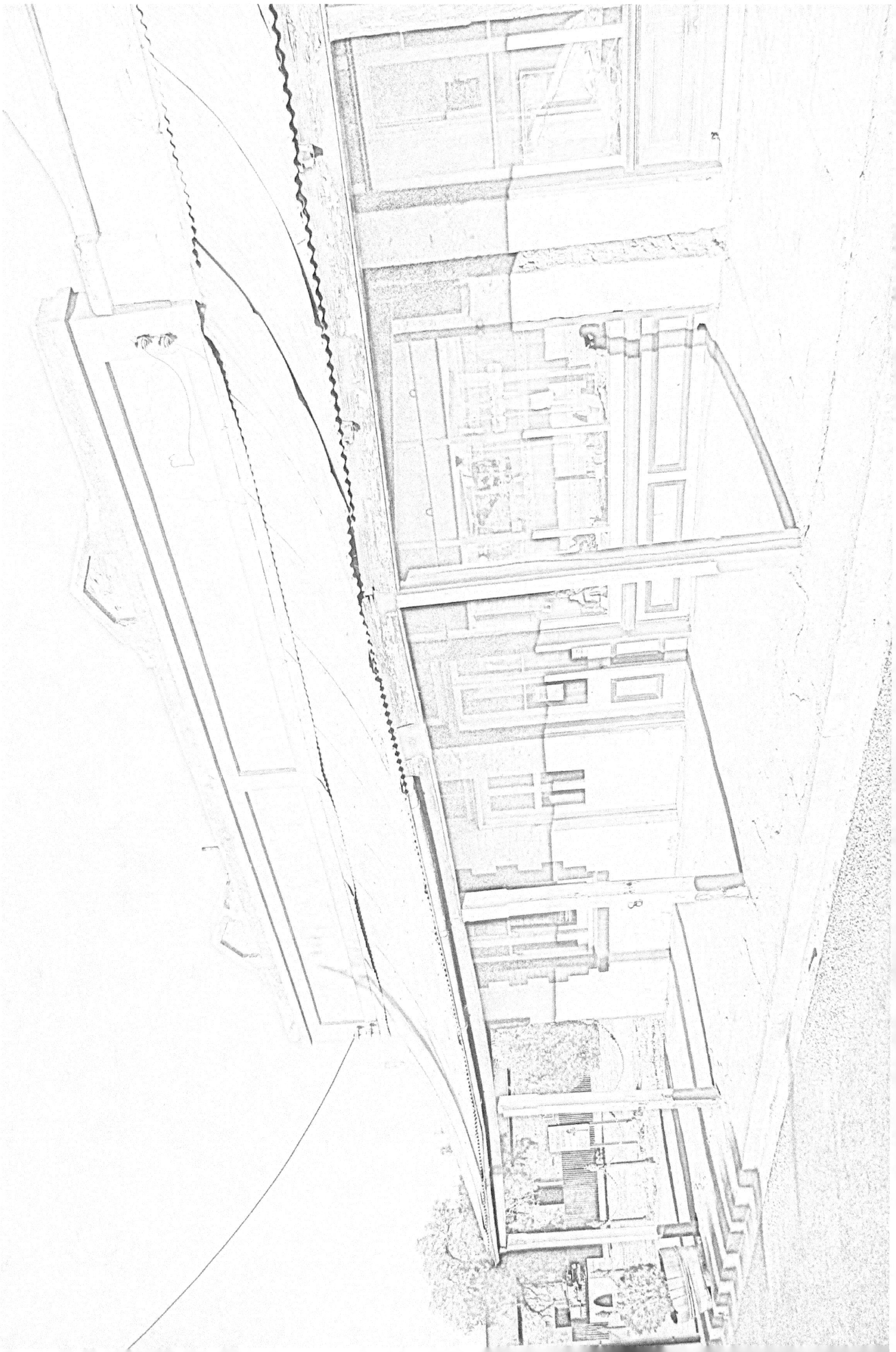

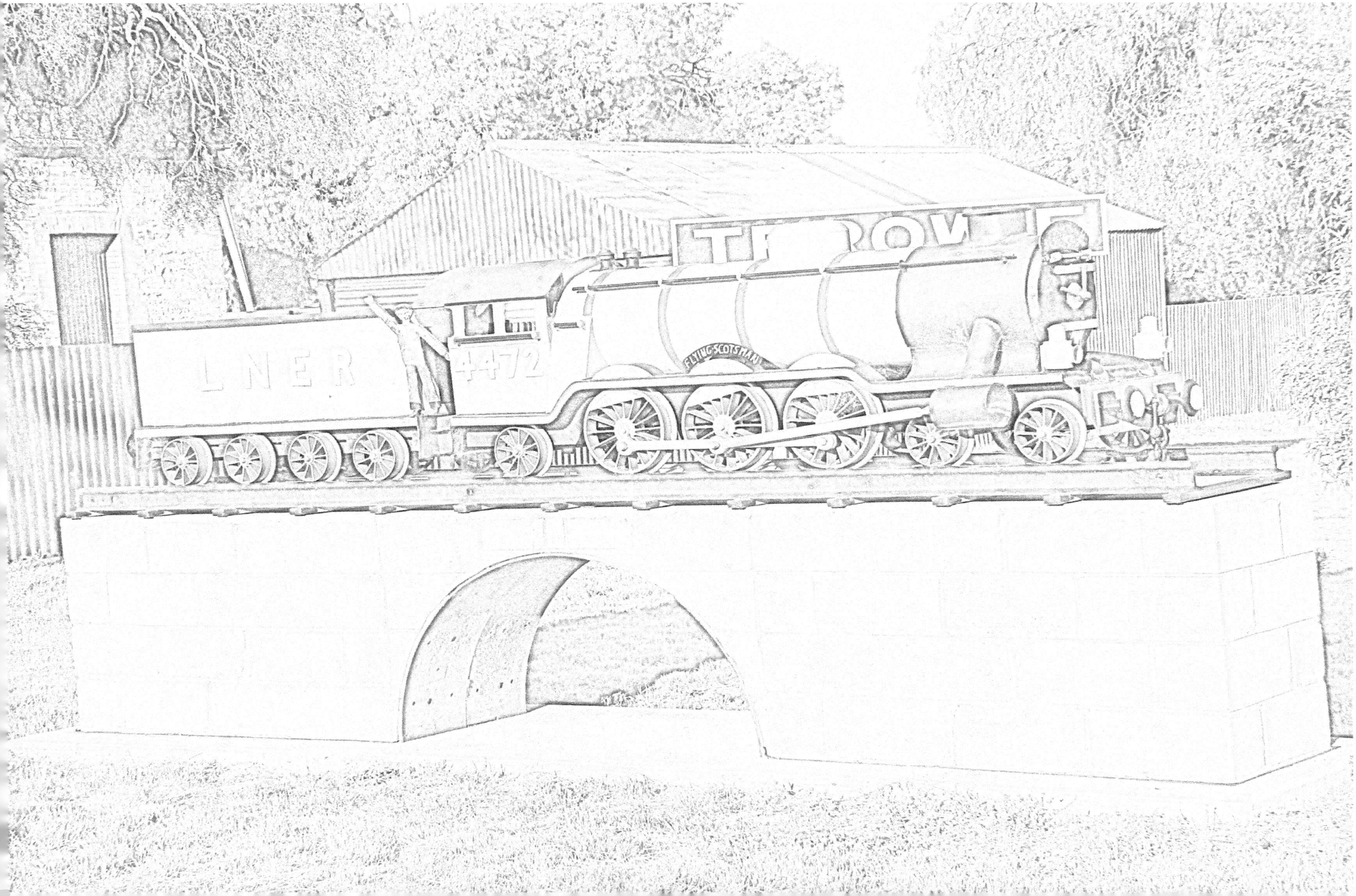
LNER
4472
FLYING SCOTSMAN

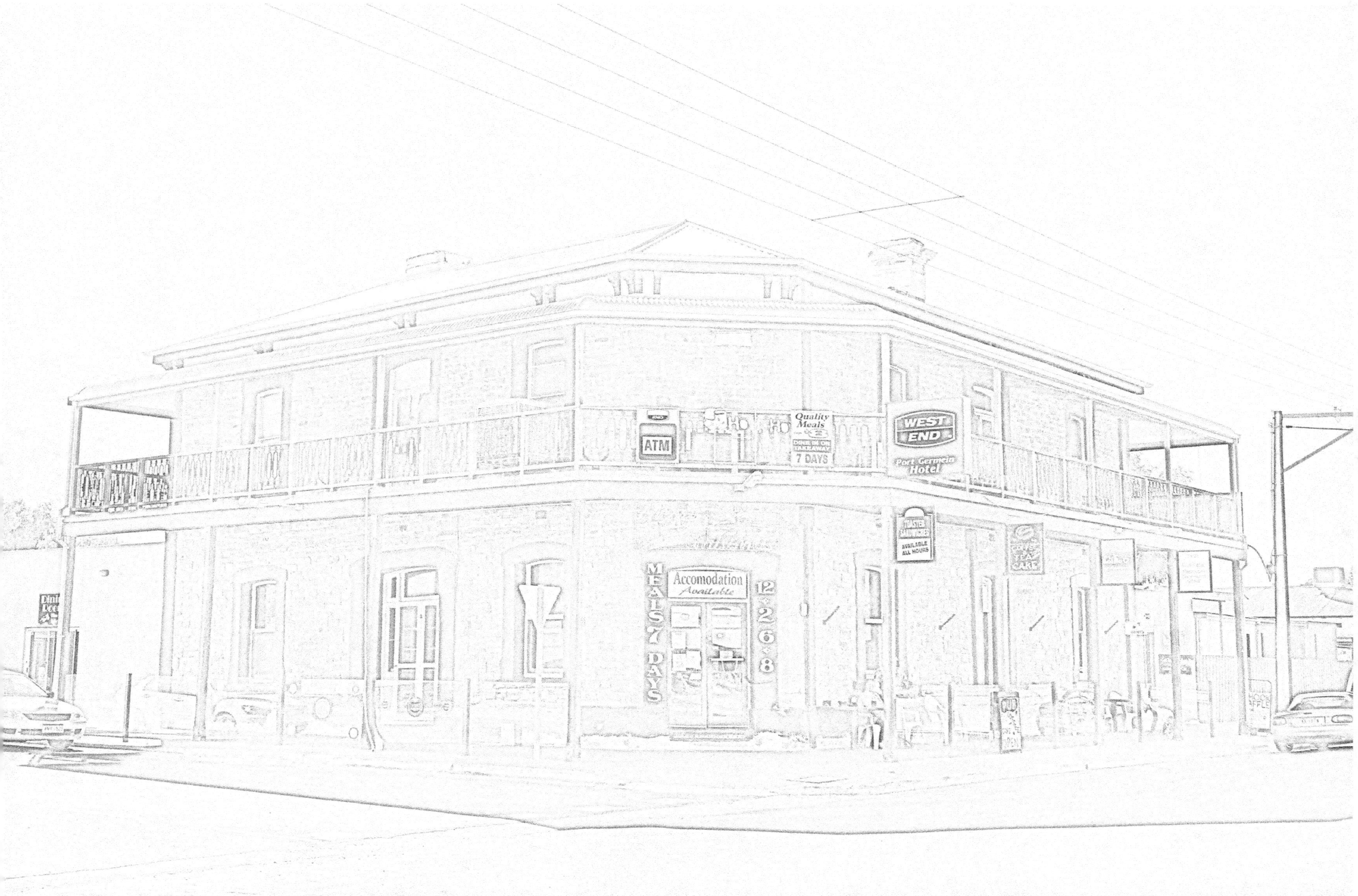
ATM
Quality Meals
DINE IN OR TAKEAWAY
7 DAYS
WEST END
Port Germein Hotel
AVAILABLE ALL HOURS
Accomodation Available
MEALS 7 DAYS
12 - 2
6 - 8

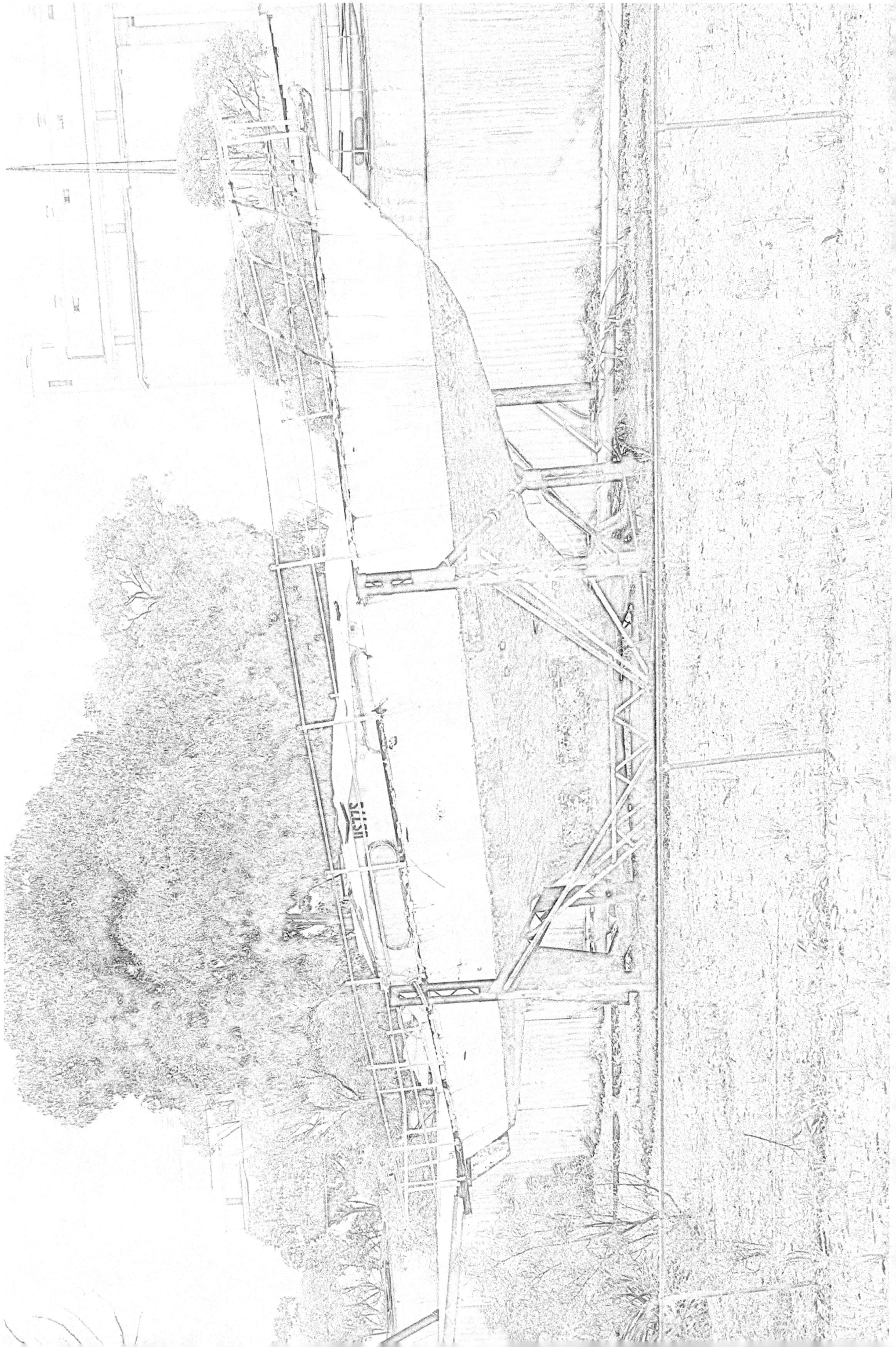

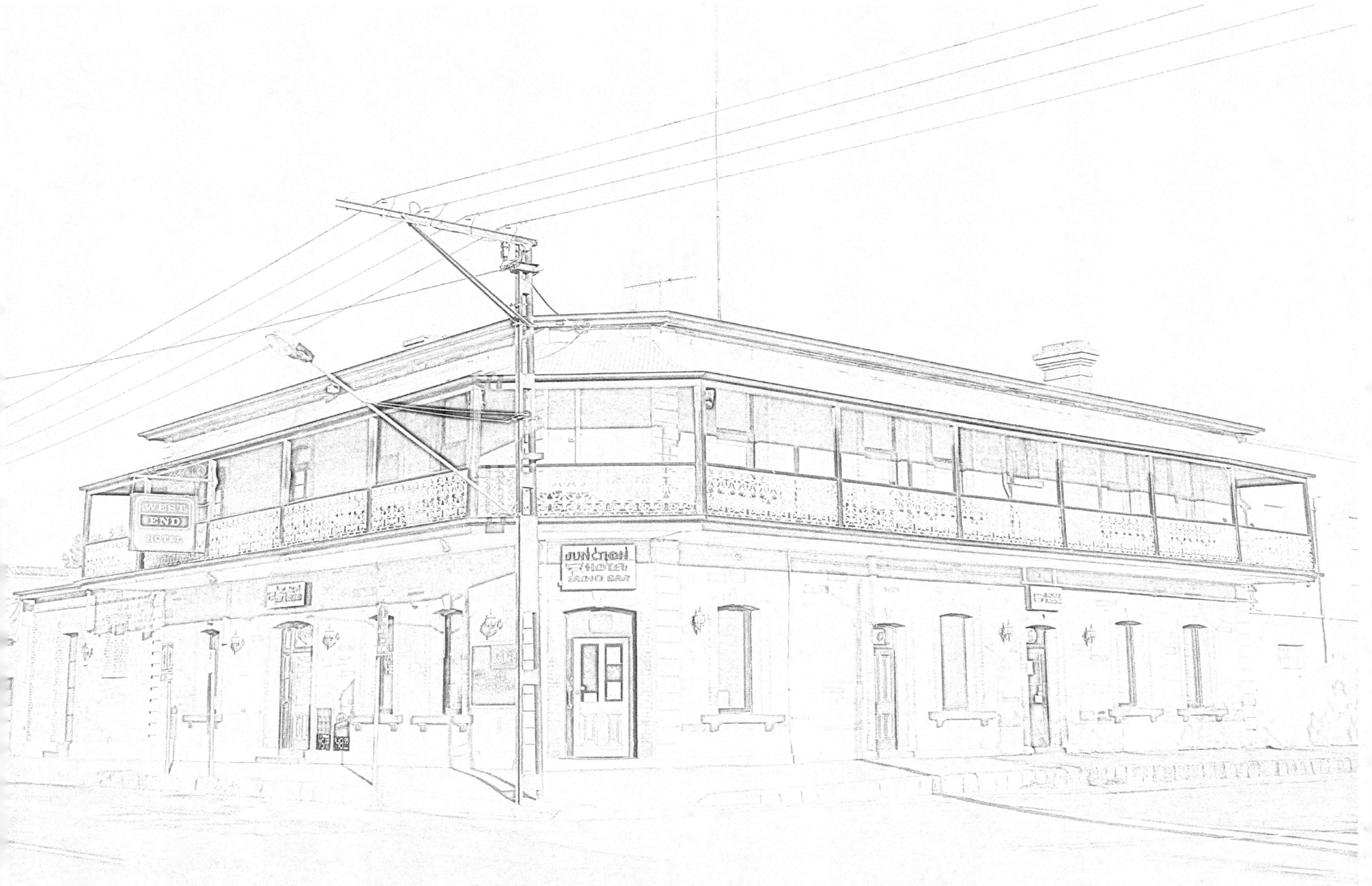
WEST END
HOTEL
JUNCTION
HOTEL

FOOD
PETERBOROUGH
HOTEL
ACCOMMODATION
WEST END
Peterborough Hotel
WEST END
WEST END
POKIE
ACCOMMODATION
NEW
ON TAP

RAILWAY HOTEL/MOTEL
• HOTEL ROOMS • SKY CHANNEL • LUXURY UNITS • POKIES • TAB
• MEALS 7 DAYS • FOX SPORTS & FOX FOOTY Ph: 08 8651 2427
TAB
Sip'n Save
Drive - In
Bottle Shop
WEST END
RAILWAY
HOTEL MOTEL
POKIES
MEADOWS ST
TAB
Sports BAR
TAKE AWAY
PIZZA
AVAILABLE
Ph: 8651 2427
ATM

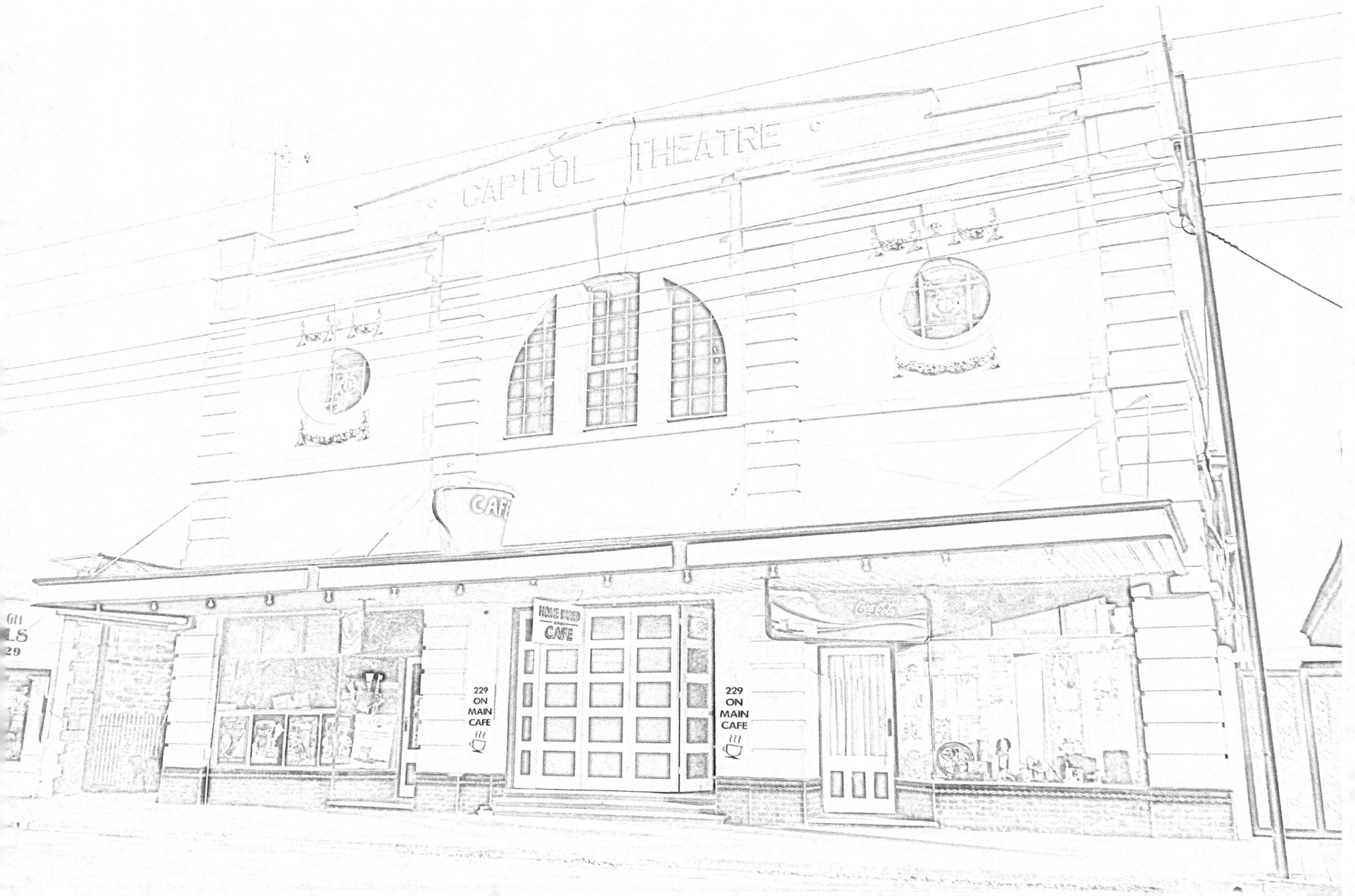
CAPITOL THEATRE
CAFE
HOME BAKED AND CAFE
229 ON MAIN CAFE
229 ON MAIN CAFE
Coca-Cola

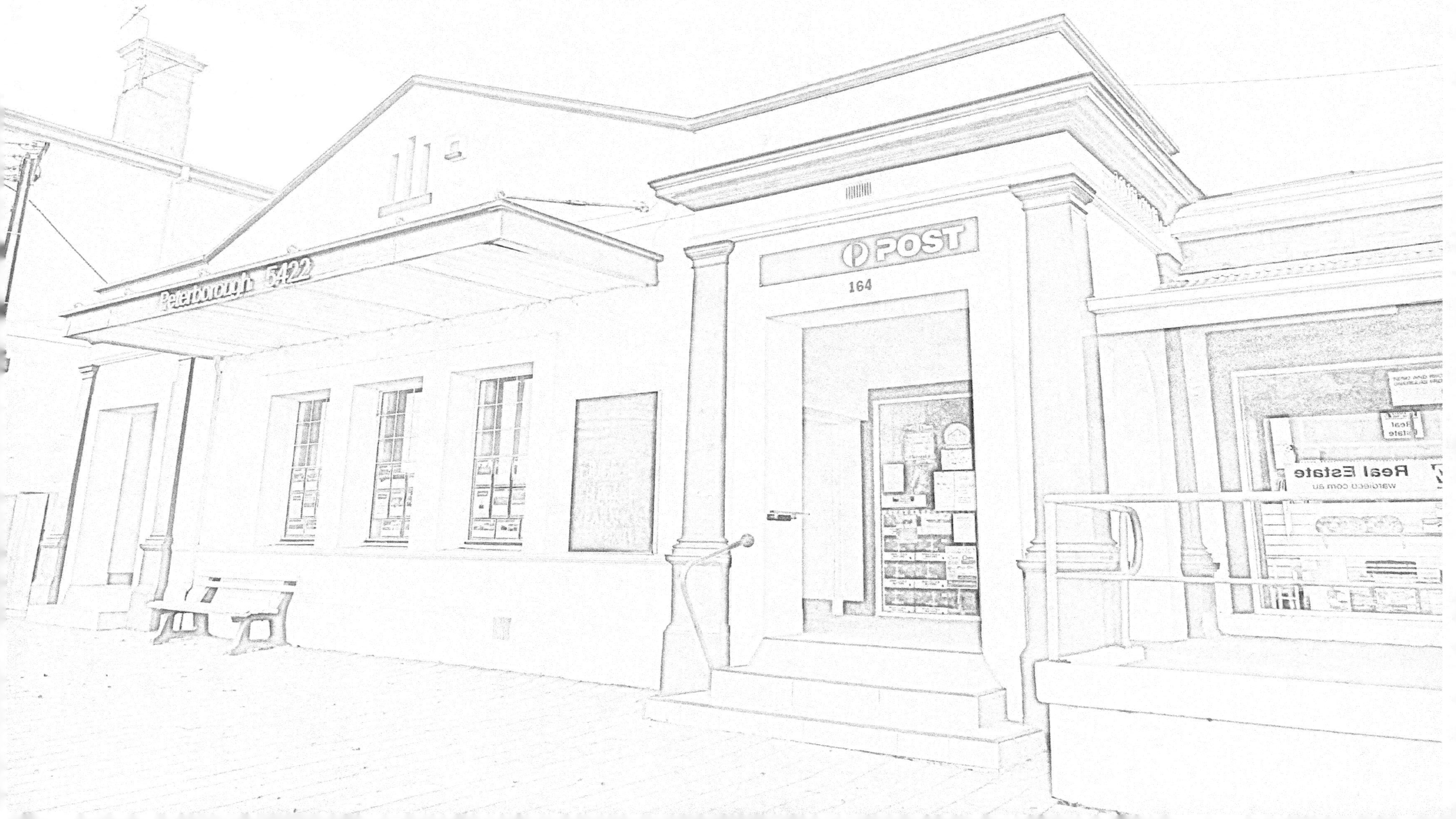
Peterborough 5422
POST
164

OLARY HOTEL
ULYSSES CLUB
WELCOME...
Bundaberg
RUM

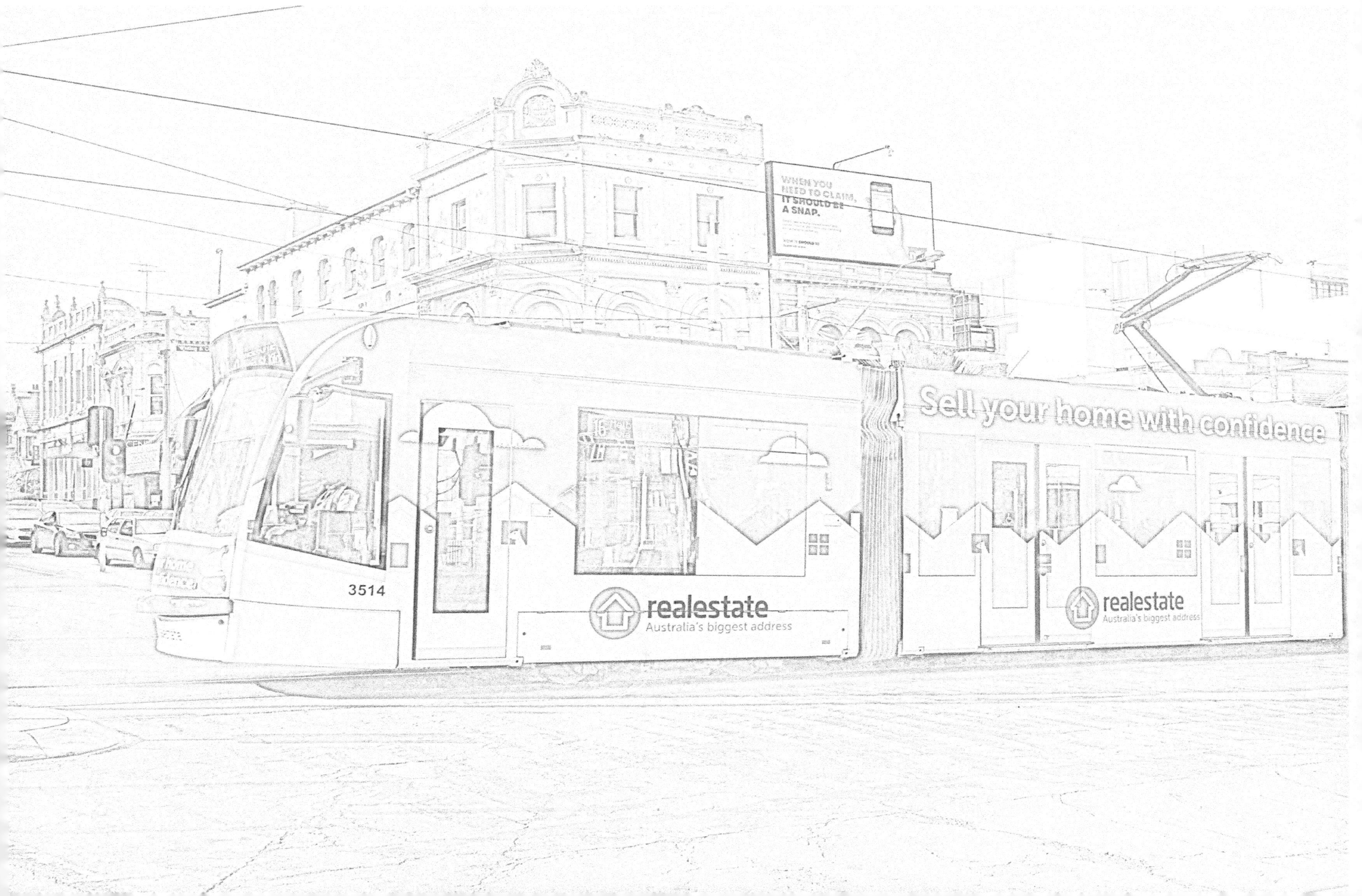
WHEN YOU NEED TO CLAIM, IT SHOULD BE A SNAP.
3514
realestate
Australia's biggest address
Sell your home with confidence
realestate
Australia's biggest address

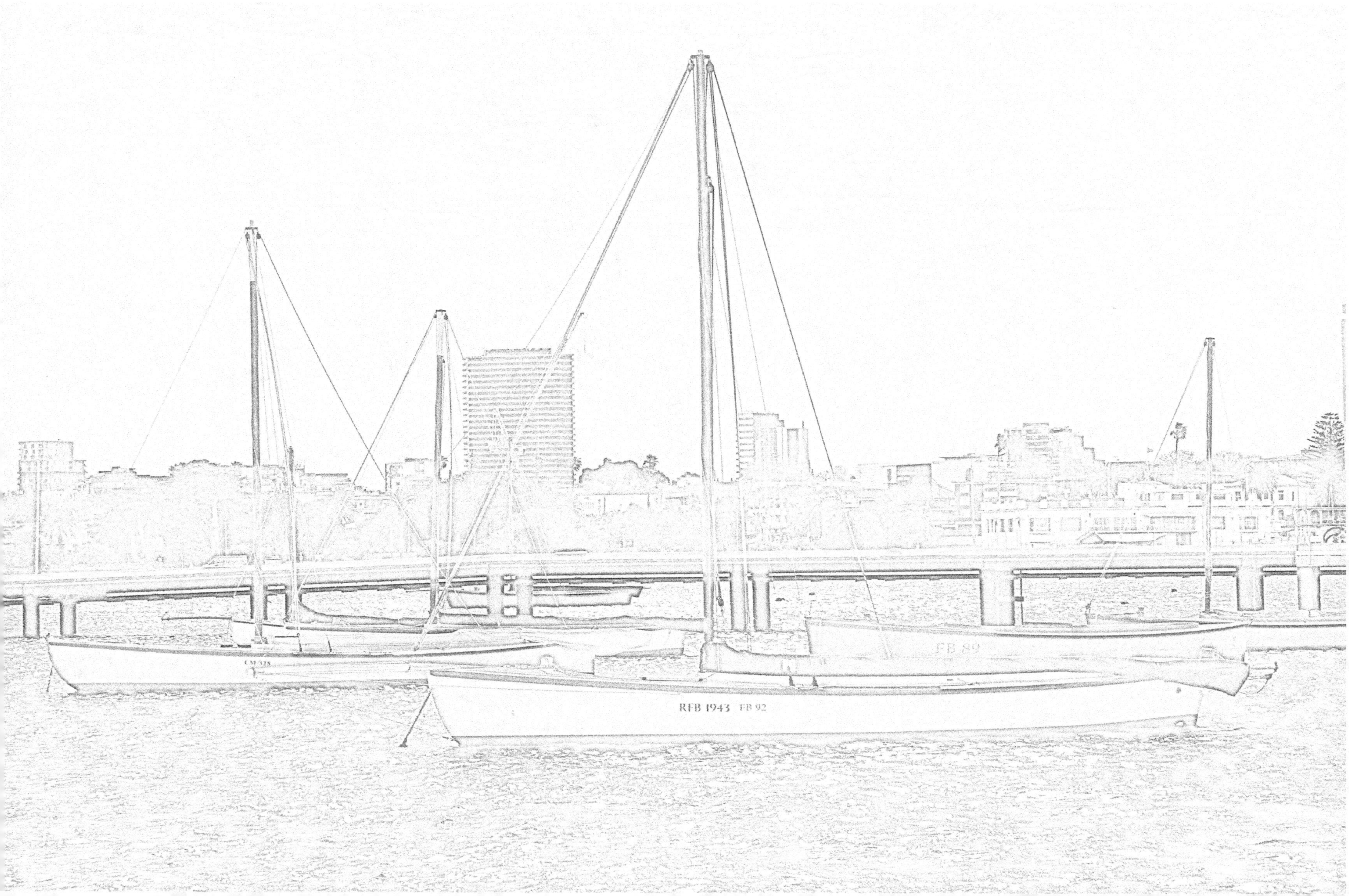
FB 89
RFB 1943 FB 92

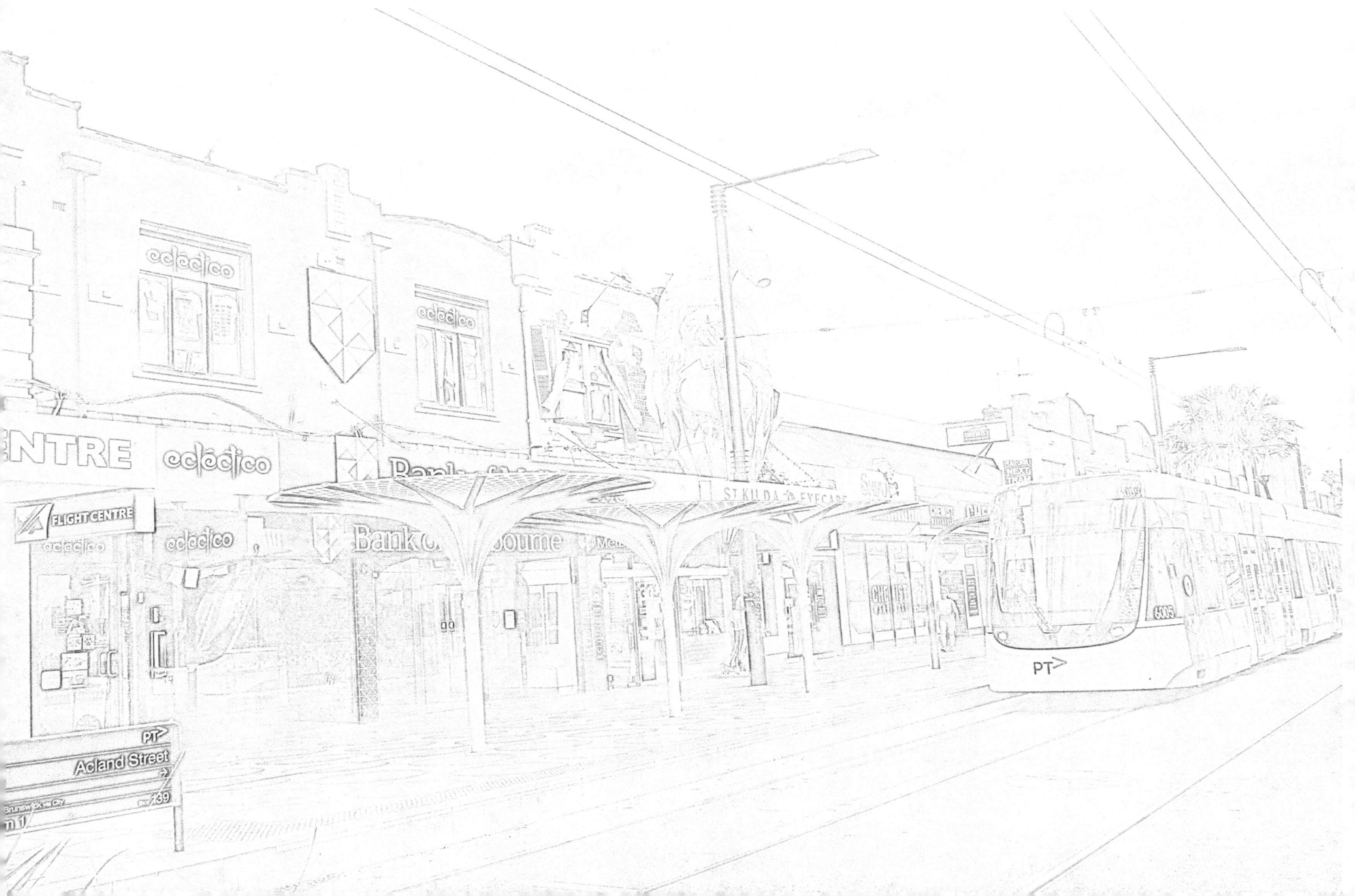
NTRE
eclectico
eclectico
eclectico
eclectico
eclectico
FLIGHT CENTRE
ST KILDA EYECARE
PT>
6005
PT>
Acland Street

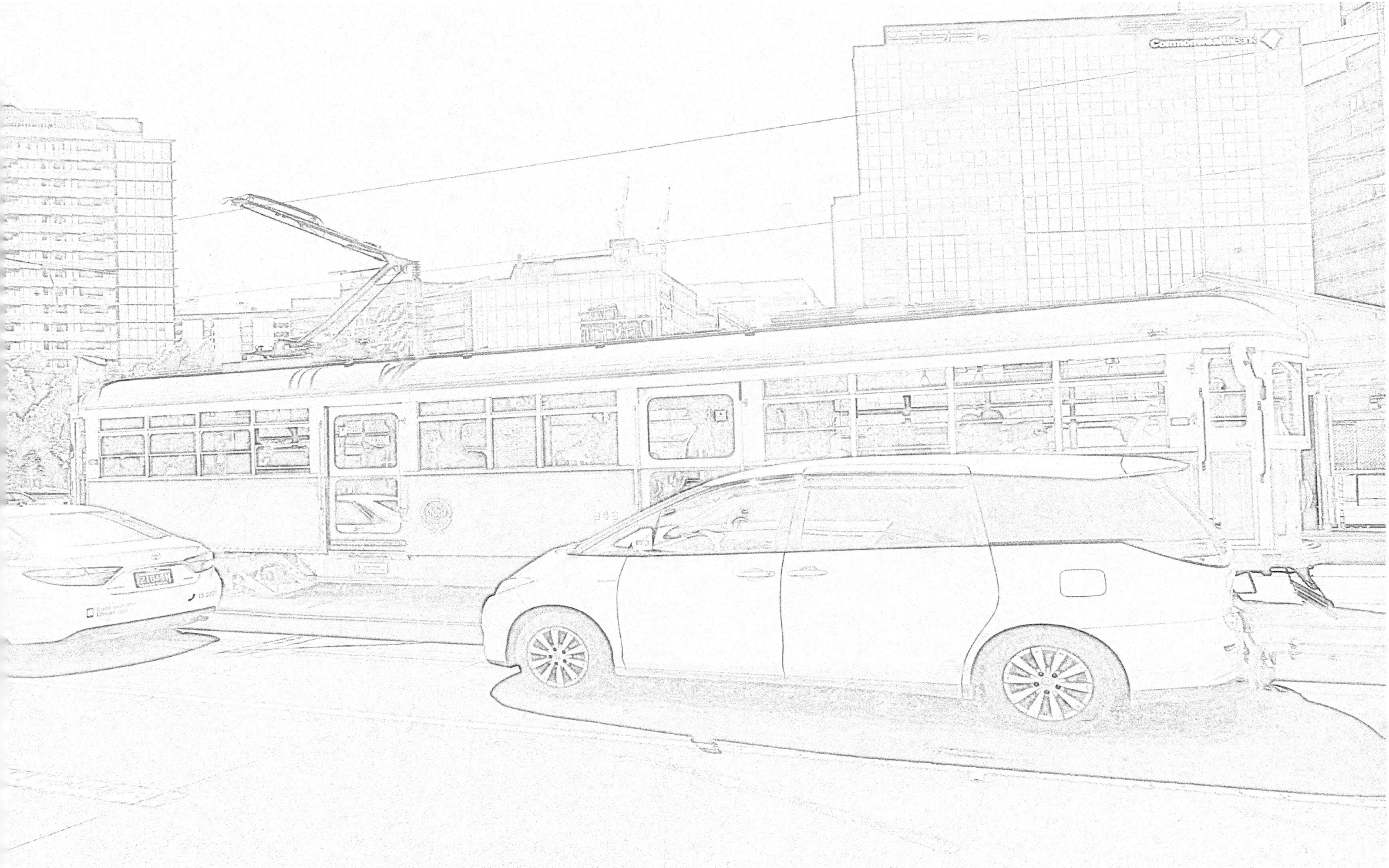
CommonwealthBank

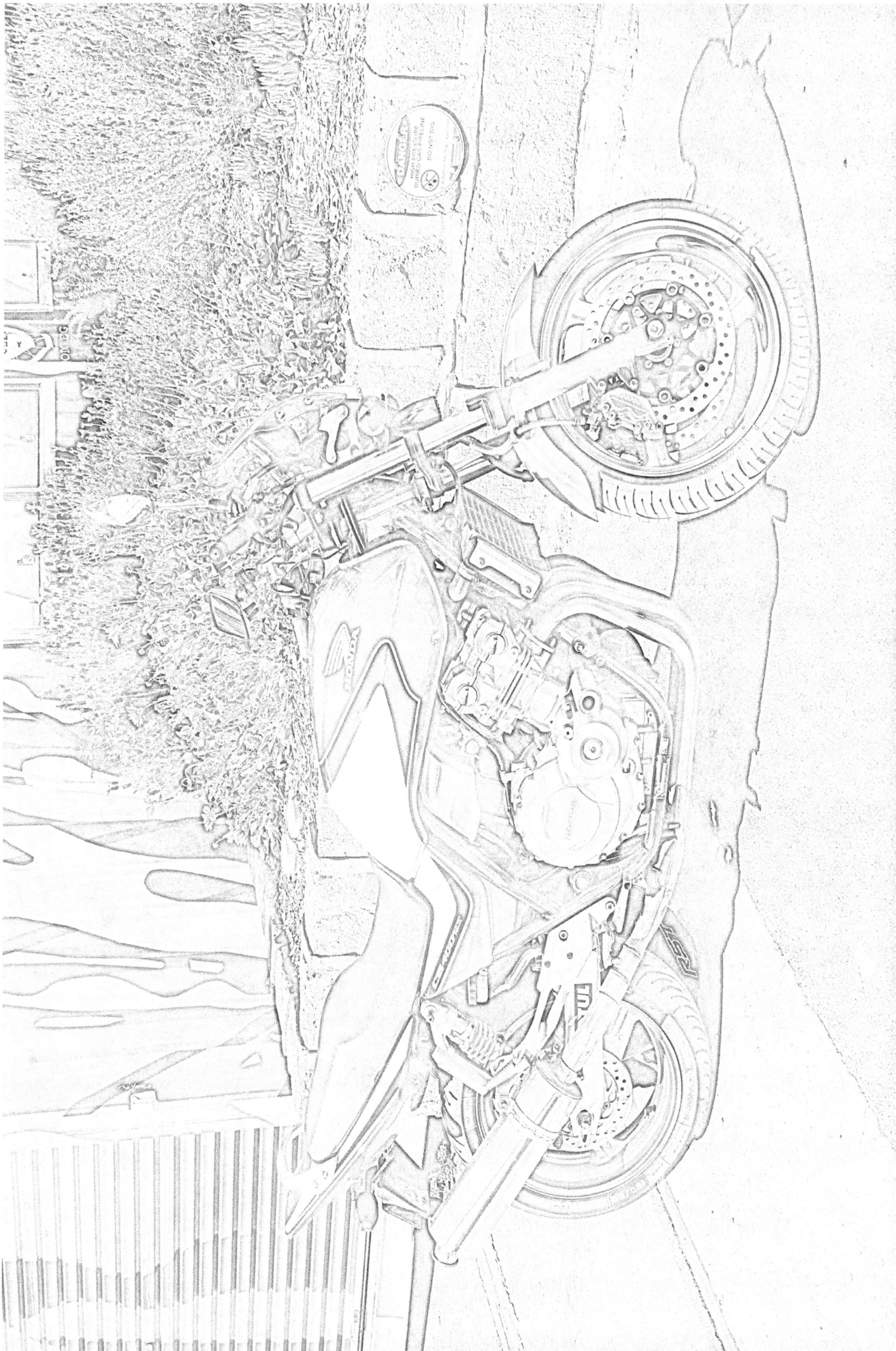
DANGER
HIGH PRESSURE
BURIED GAS PIPELINE
DO NOT DIG

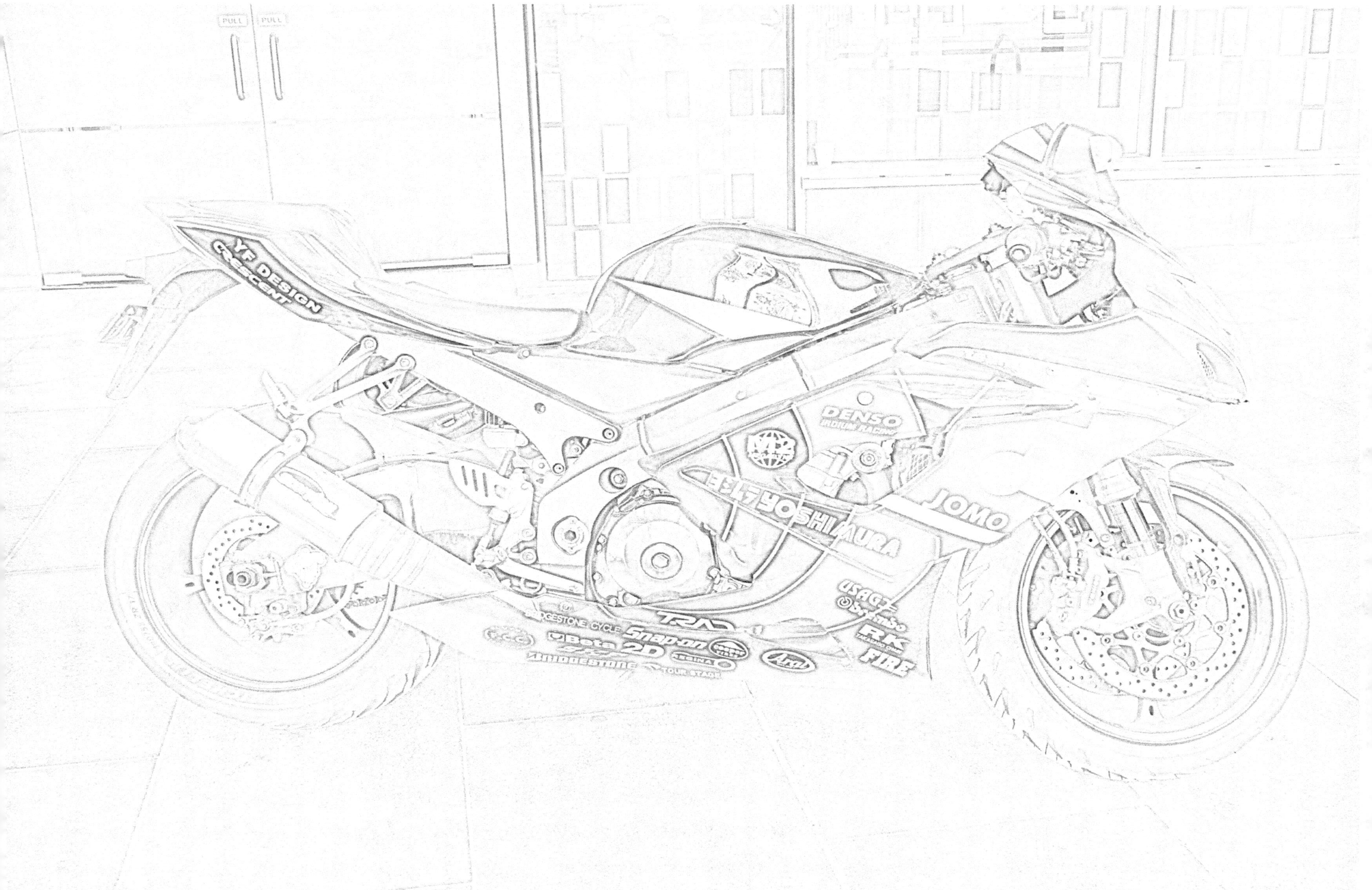
PULL
PULL
YF DESIGN
CRESCENT
DENSO
YOSHIMURA
JOMO
TRAD
Snap-on
Beta
2D
BRIDGESTONE
TOUR STAGE
FIRE

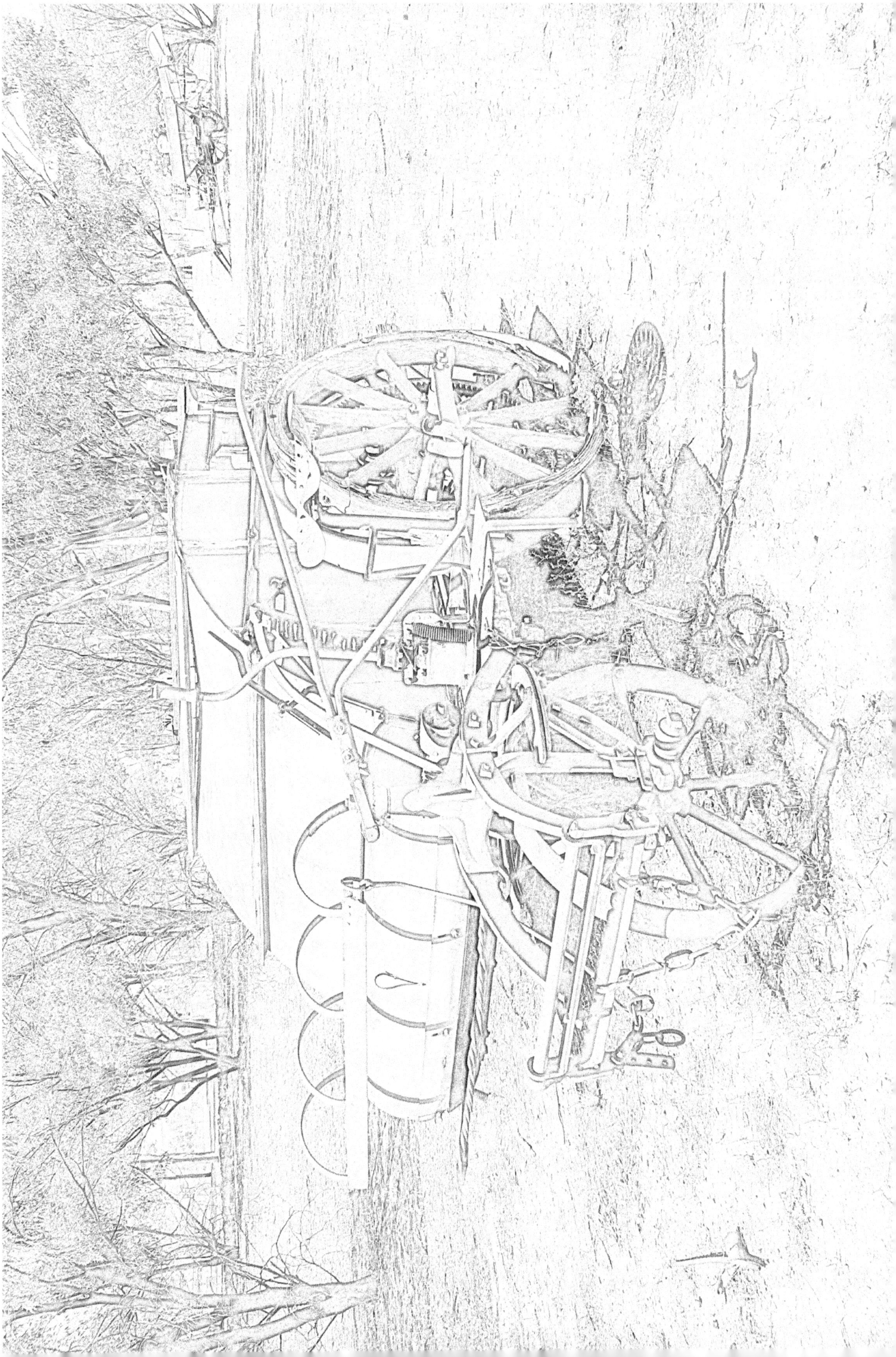

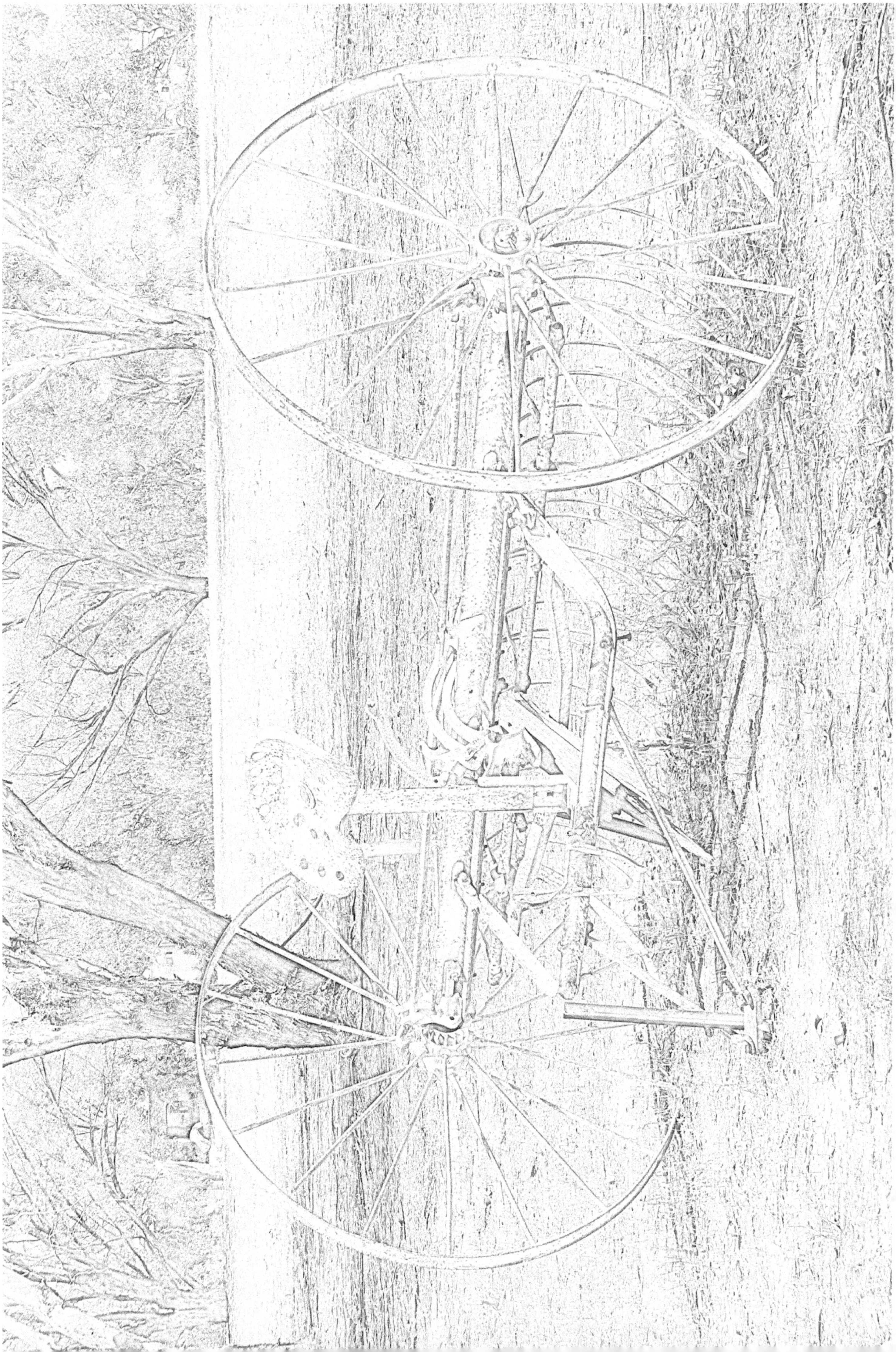

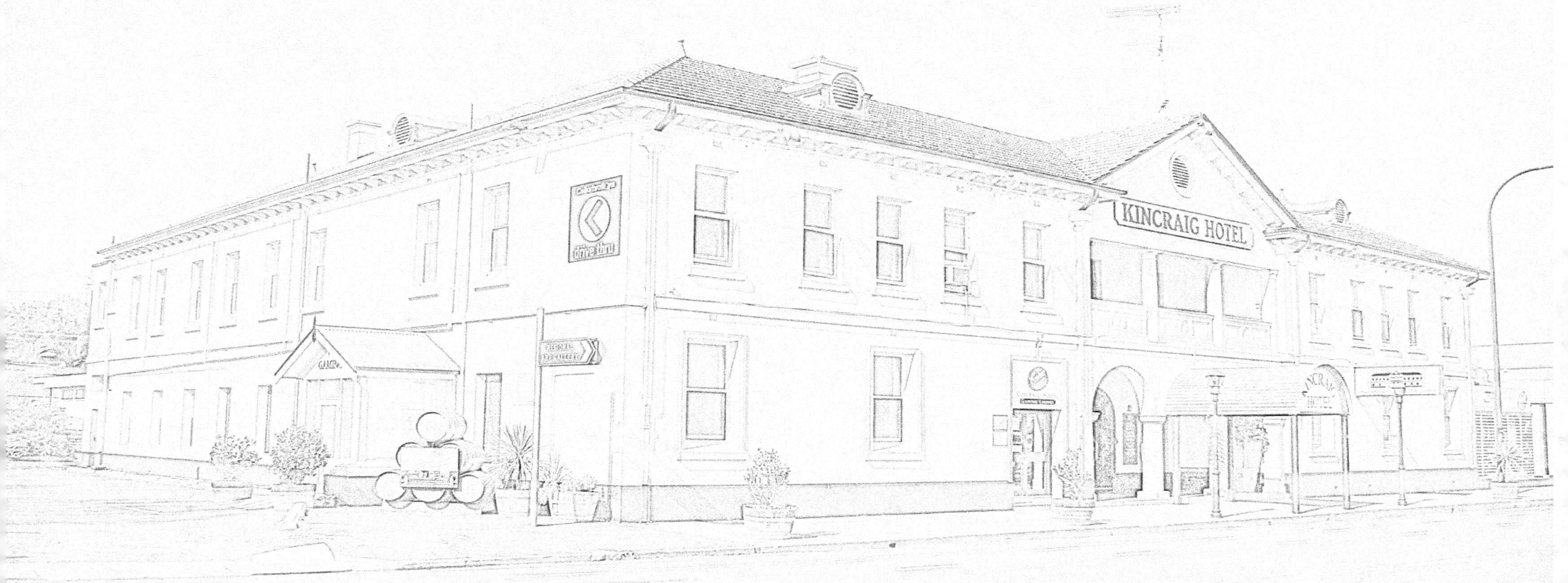
KINCRAIG HOTEL
drive thru
KINCRAIG HOTEL

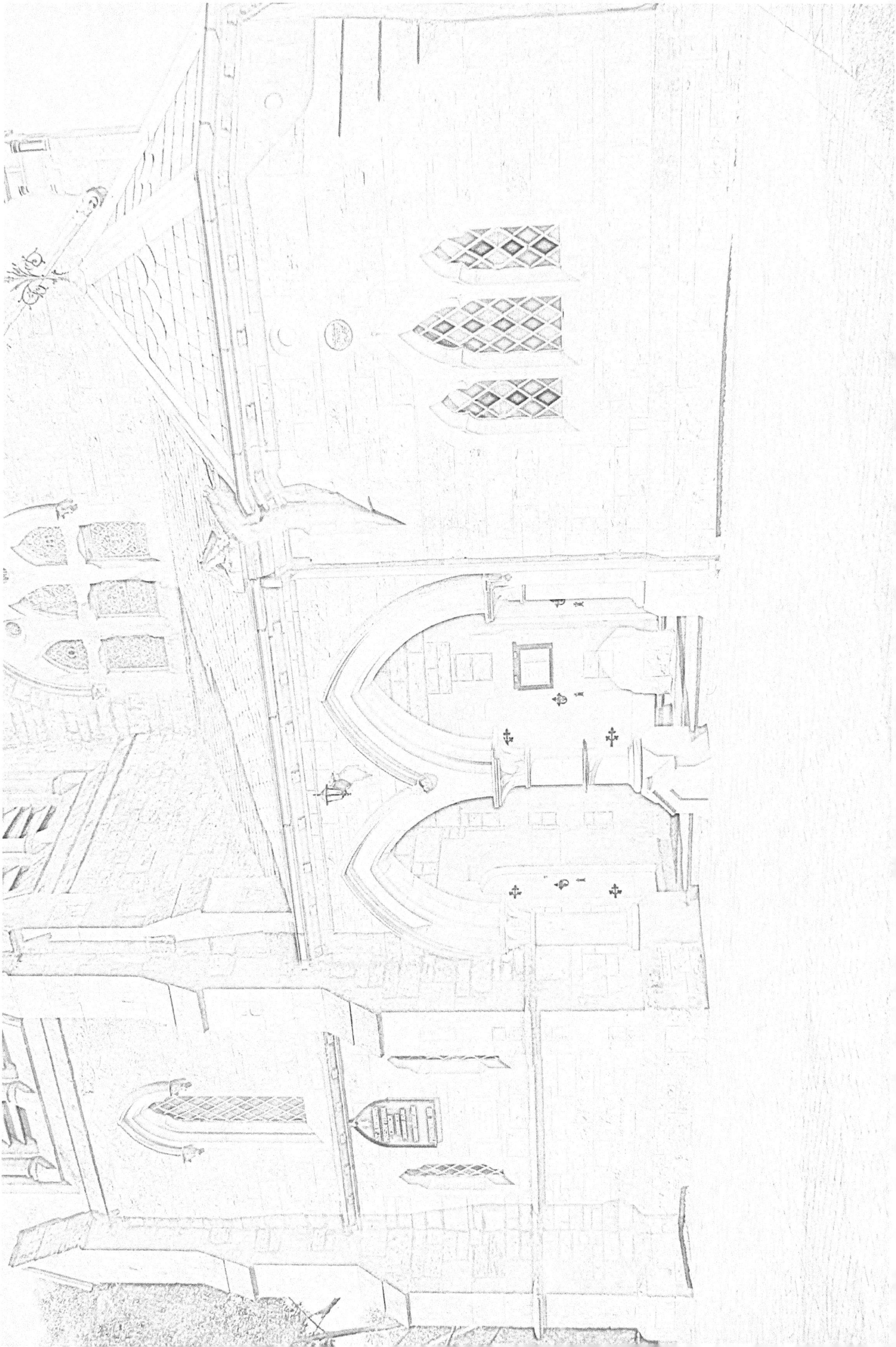

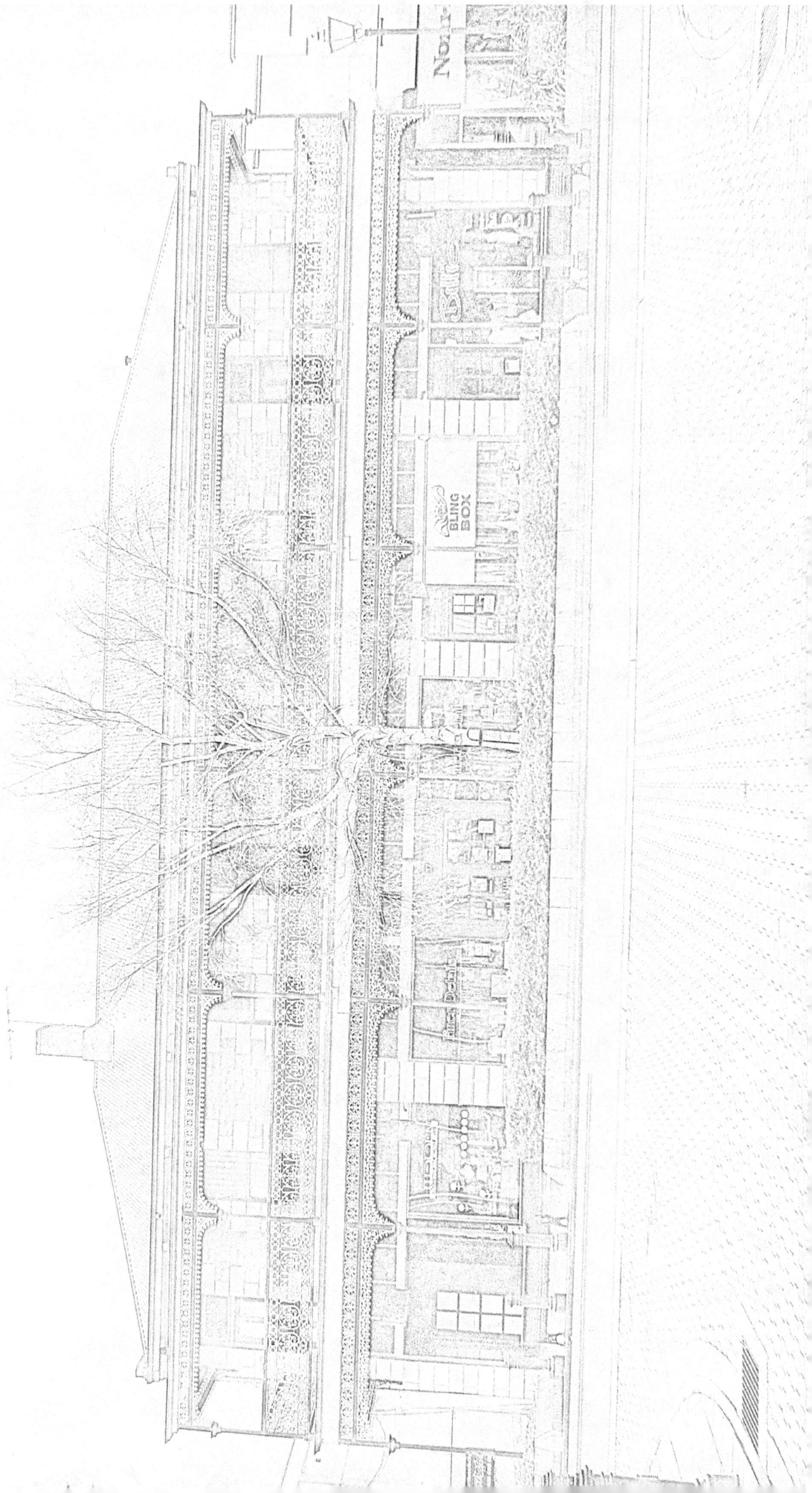
BLING BOX

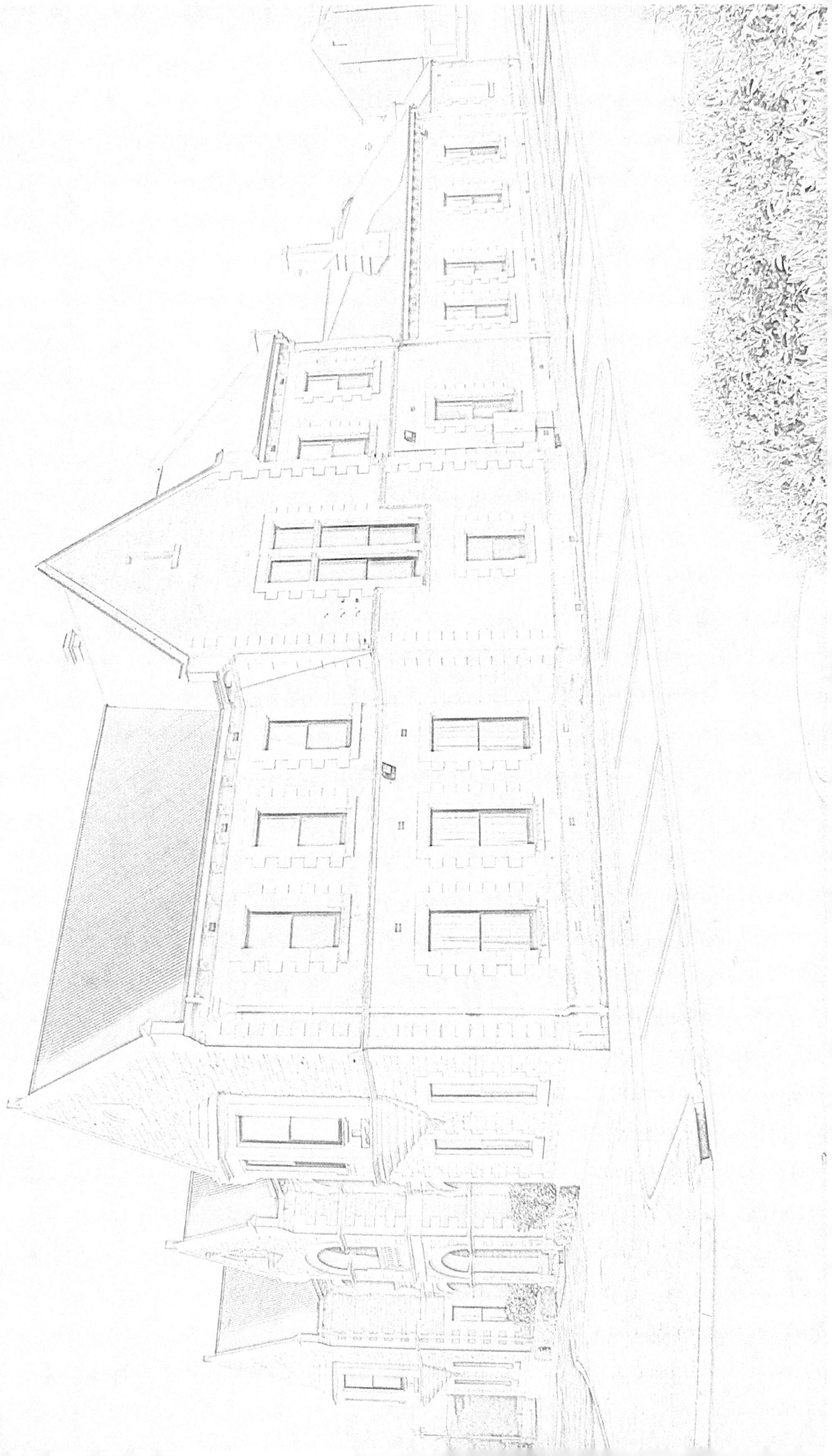

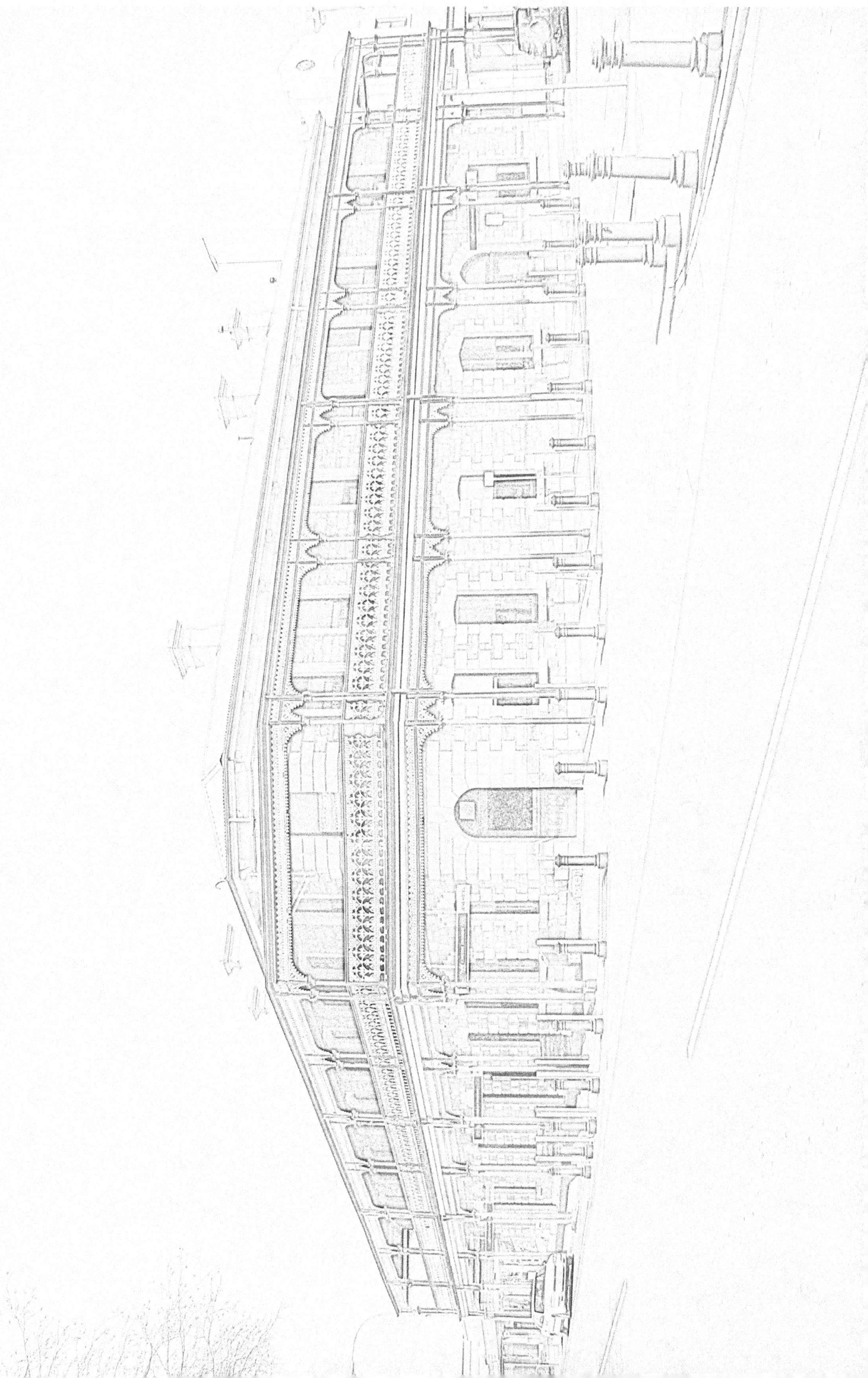

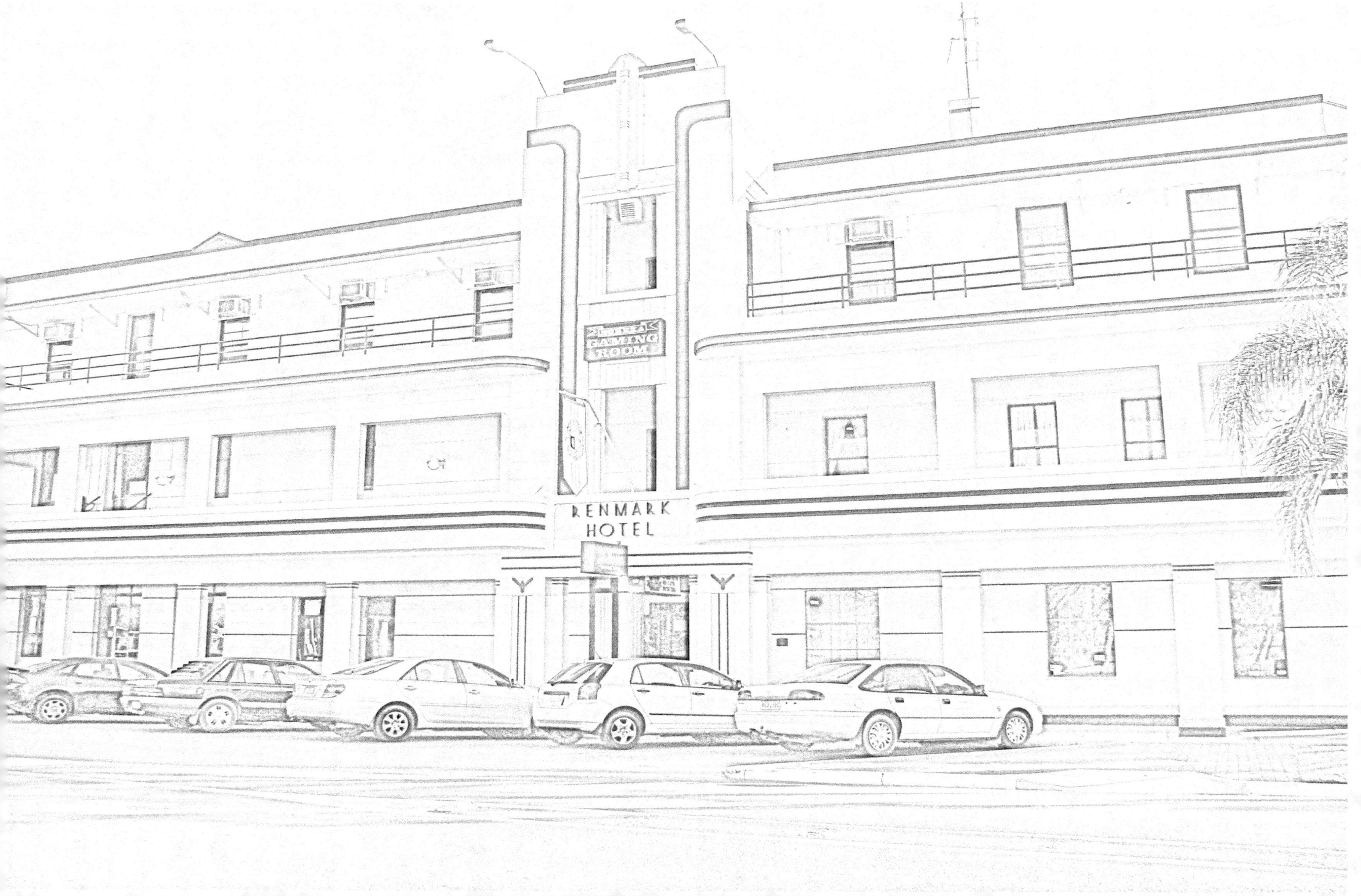
RENMARK
HOTEL
GAMING
ROOM

EST. 1878
TAKE AWAY FOOD, PIZZA BAR
ICE, SOUVENIRS, DRINKS
Morgan Riverview Cafe
Now Open
RIVERLAND
ICE
OPEN

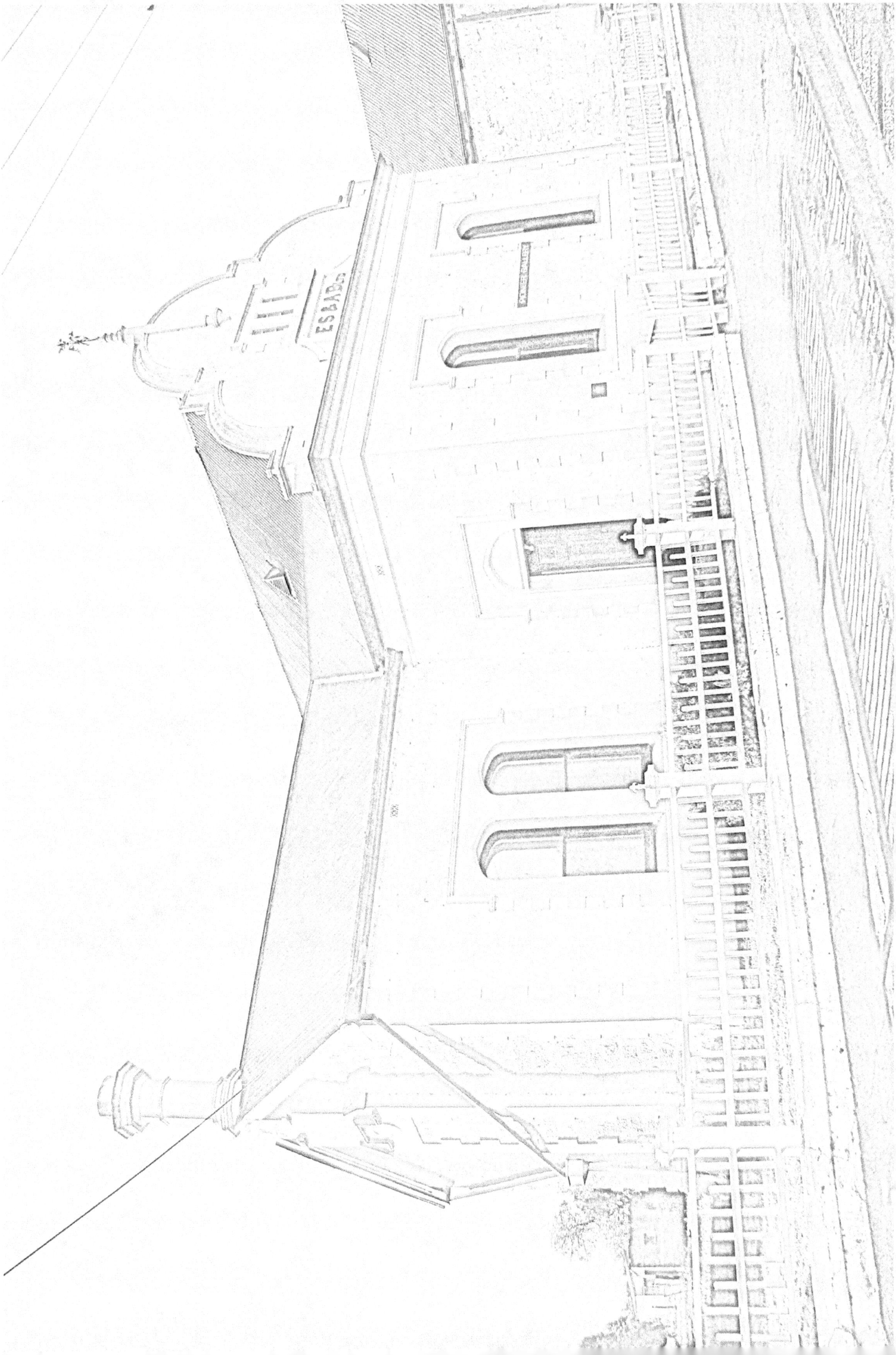

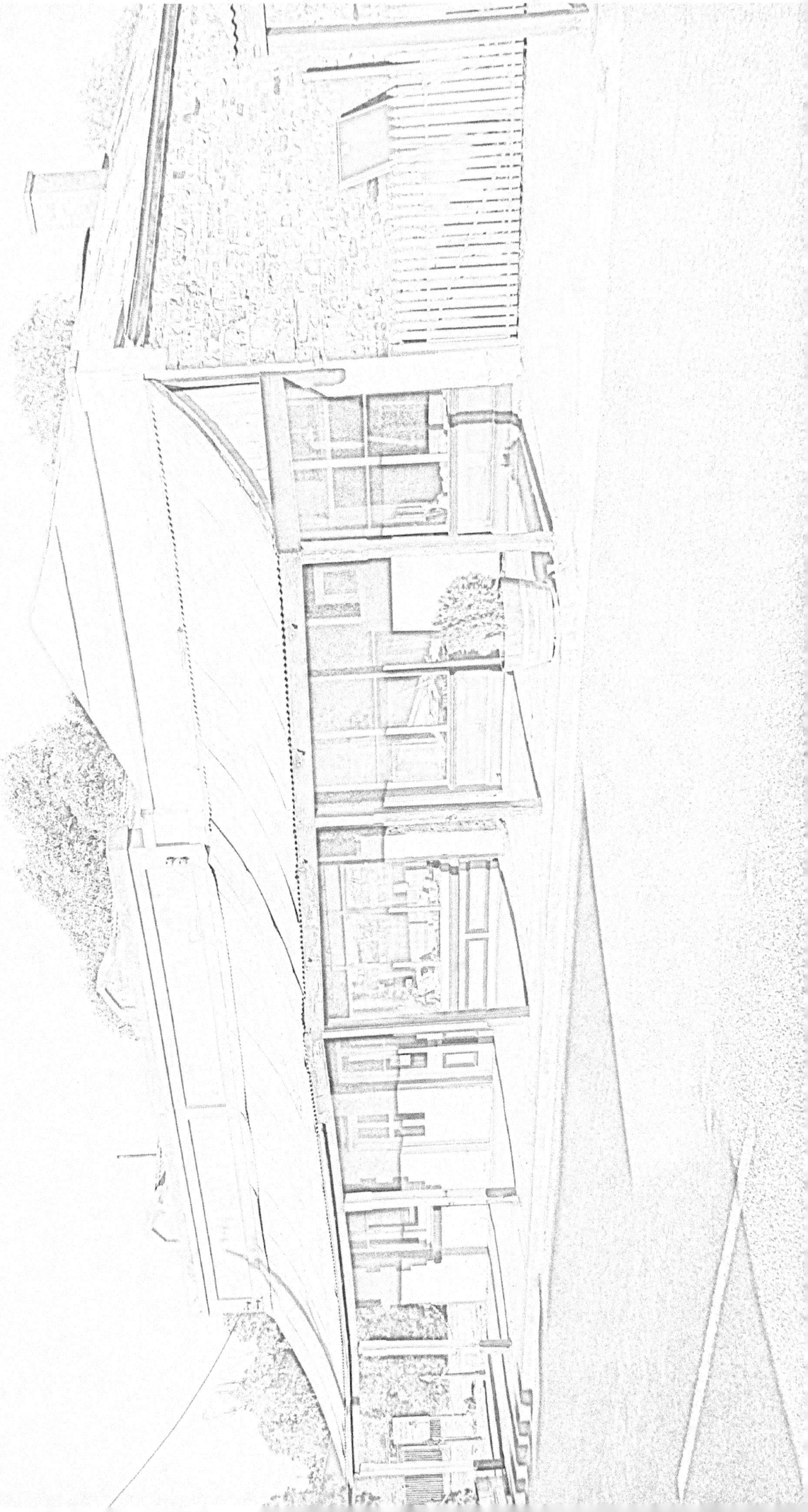

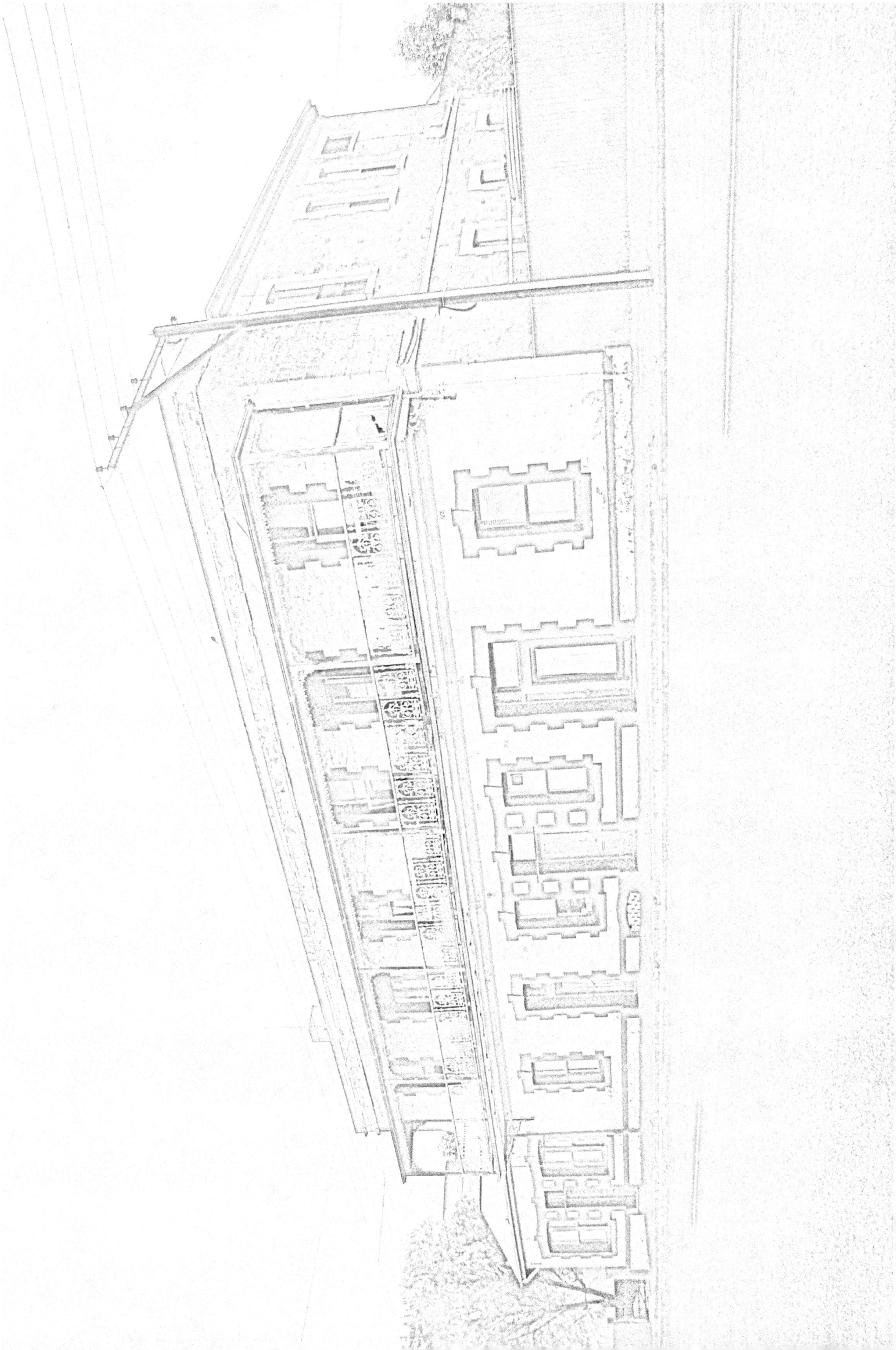

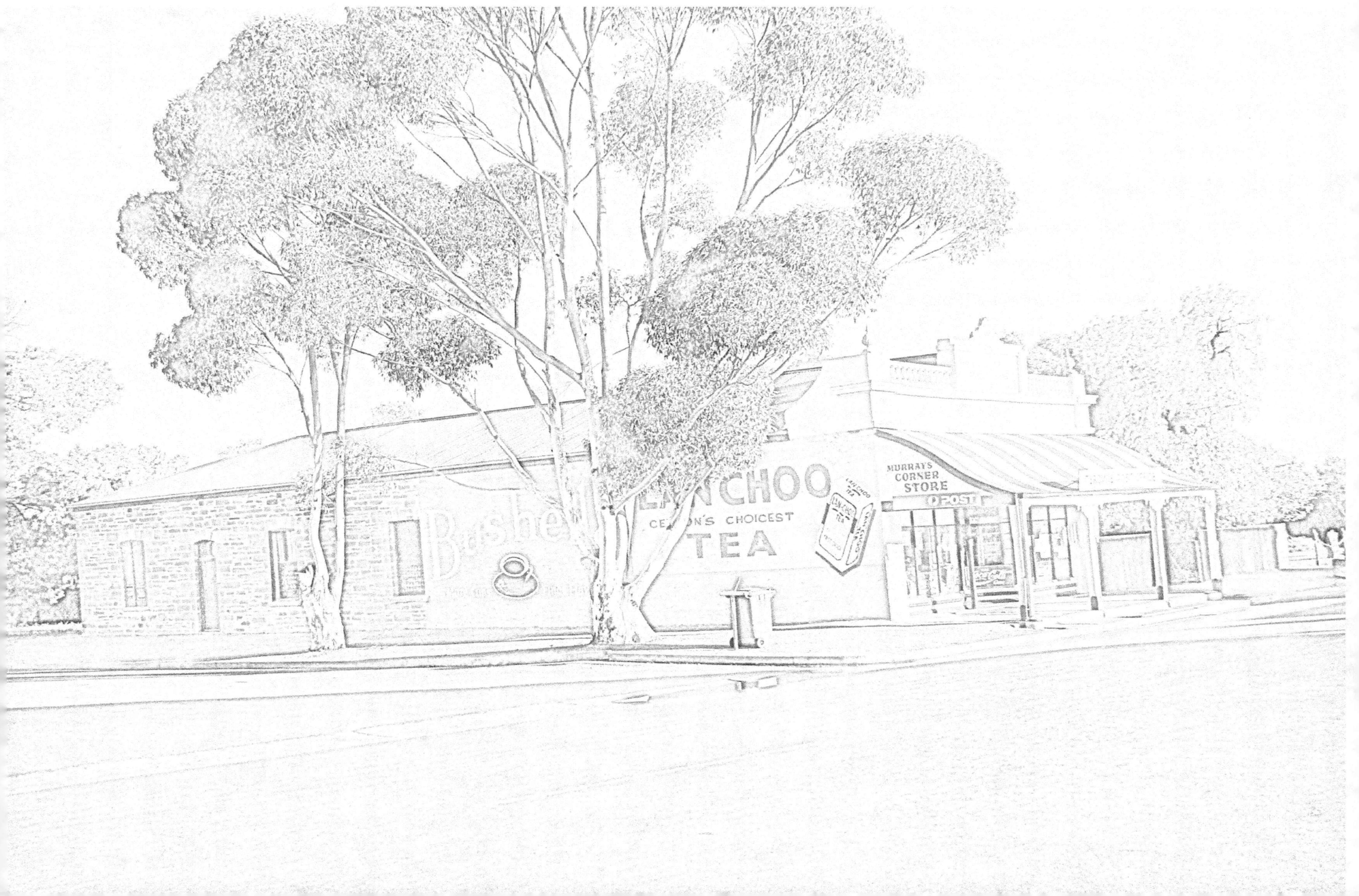
CHOICEST
TEA
MURRAYS
CORNER
STORE
POST

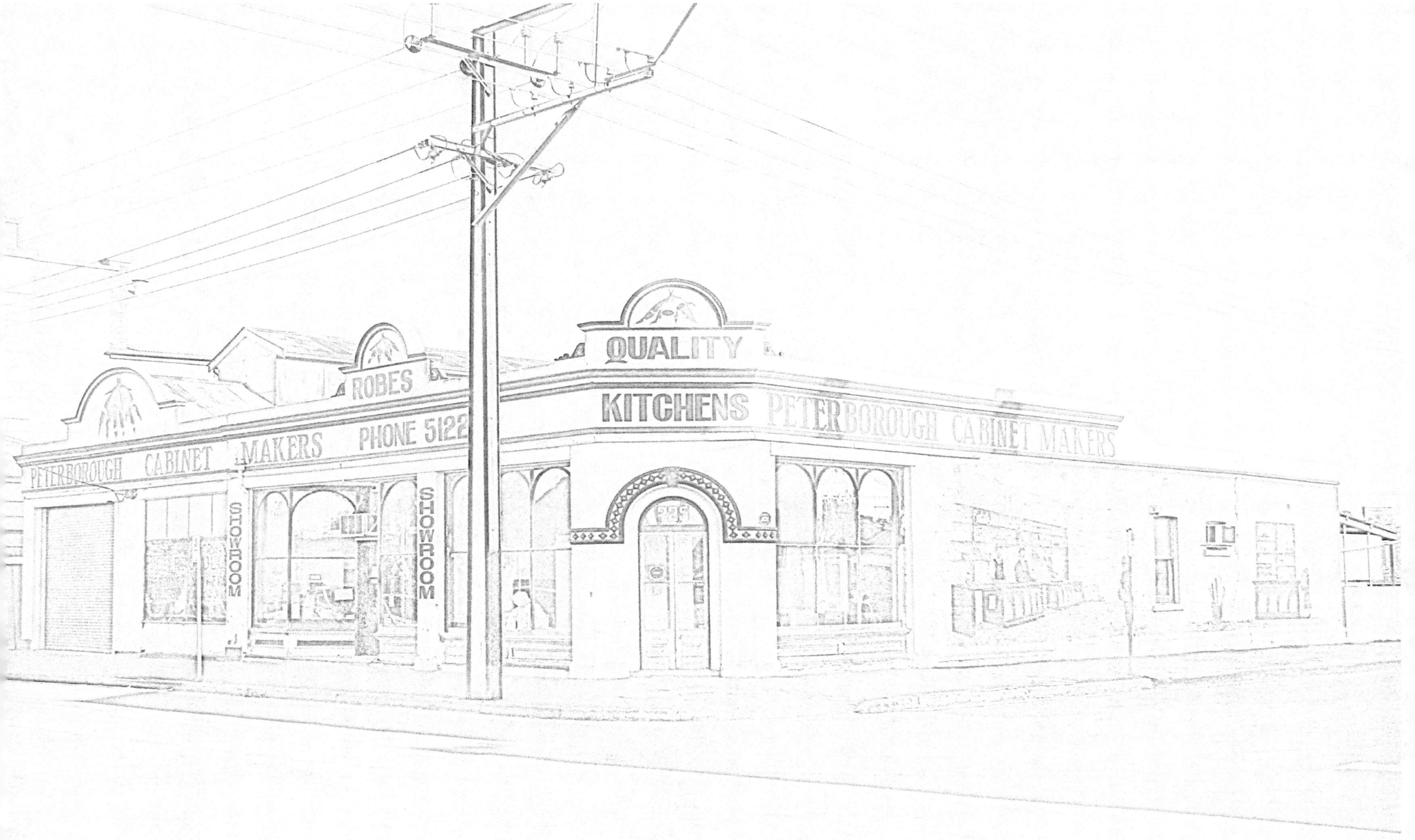
QUALITY
ROBES
KITCHENS
PETERBOROUGH CABINET MAKERS
PHONE 5122
PETERBOROUGH CABINET MAKERS
SHOWROOM
SHOWROOM

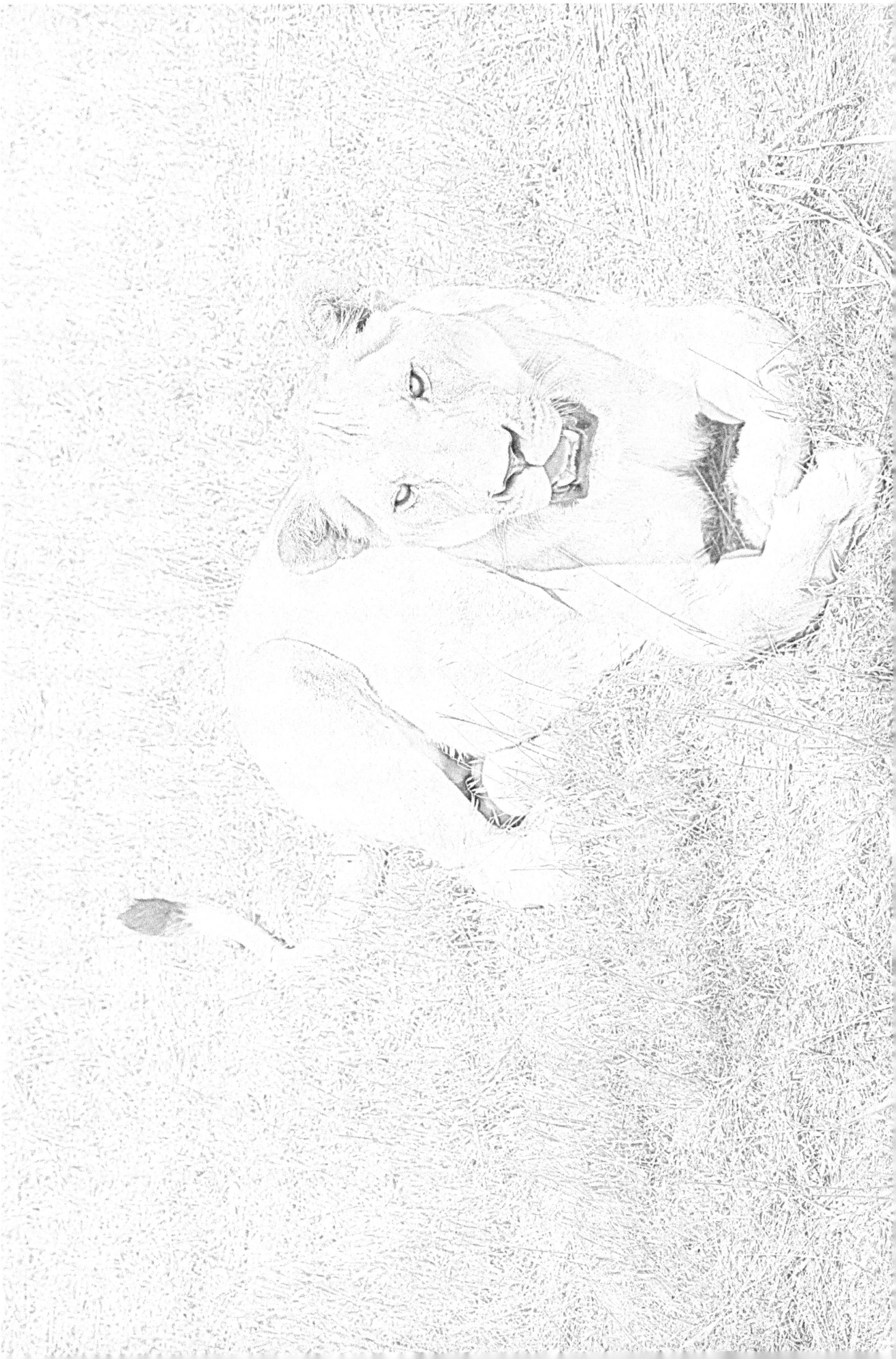

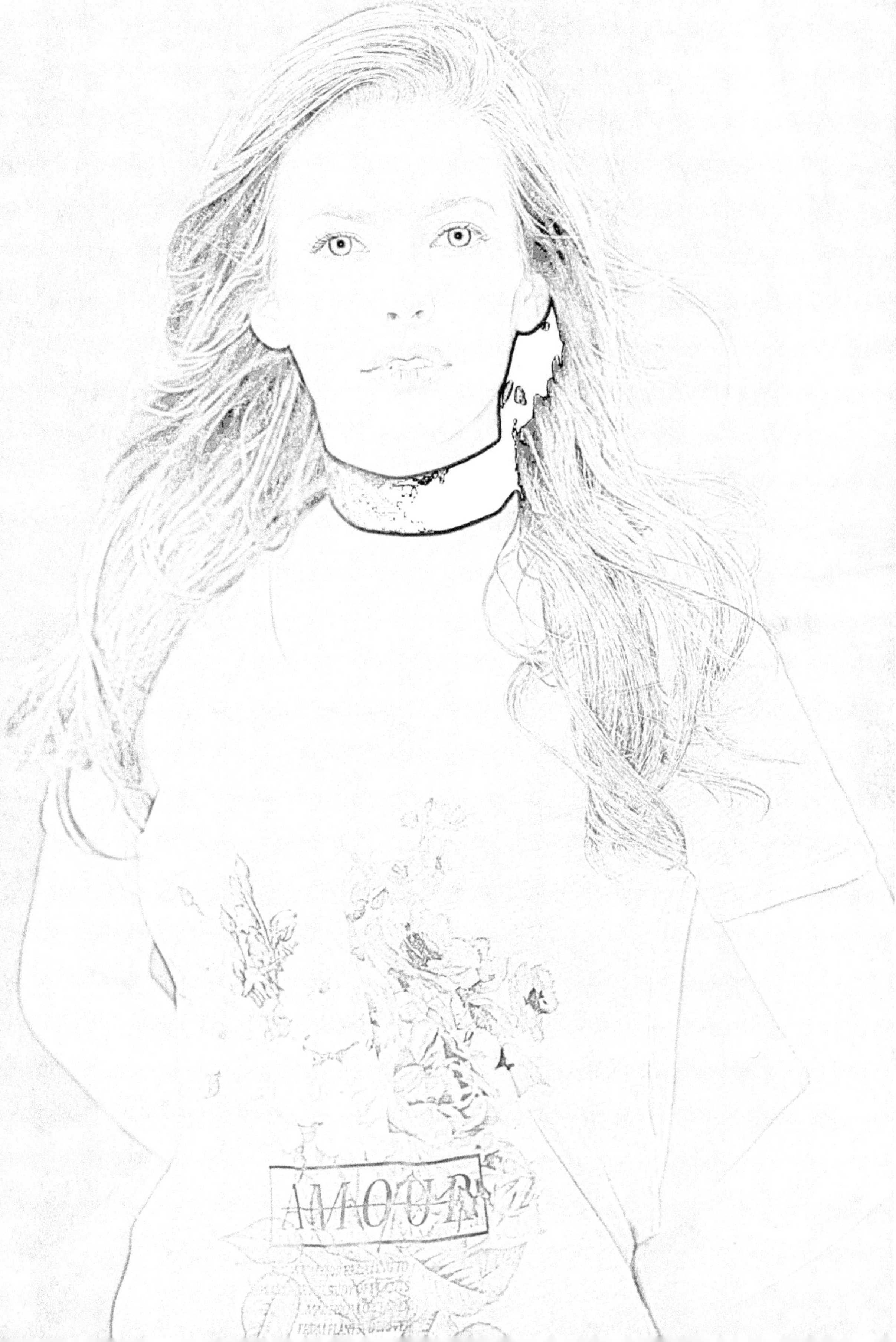
AMOUR

www.ingramcontent.com/pod-product-compliance
Lightning Source LLC
Chambersburg PA
CBHW081100180526
45170CB00005B/1826